GREENBOOK ®

Guide to

Department 56 ® INC.

Snowbabies™

1998/1999 Edition

The Most Respected Guides To Contemporary Collectibles
& Their After Market Values

2000 Sunset Drive, P.O. Box 645
Pacific Grove, CA 93950
408.656.9000
FAX 408.656.9004
http://www.greenbooks.com

Printed in Canada

ISBN 0-923628-54-1

The GREENBOOK would like to thank…

Department 56, Inc.

The collectors, retailers, secondary market dealers and newsletter publishers across the country who take their valuable time to supply us with information, including secondary market status and price.

Acknowledgments

If you own the previous edition of the GREENBOOK Guide to Department 56® Snowbabies™, you'll notice a few changes in this 1998/1999 Edition.

In response to collector requests we have increased the size of the photographs and reorganized some of the detail information.

In addition, we have added a History List that contains the total product line. Department 56, Inc. has discontinued its list and changed the format for product information. Department 56, Inc. will have an Historical Brochure which will highlight the retired pieces and a separate fact sheet for current product. These will be available at your retailer. The GREENBOOK History List puts all the information in one place, at your fingertips, for a quick check, right next to the pages of product pictures and data.

The Wishlist is now focusing only on the Porcelain Bisque Collection and incorporates color photographs. It conveniently slips into your pocket as you treasure hunt or is a great gift hint when you are hoping to receive that very special figurine.

If you'd like a Bookmark Update to keep your GREENBOOK guide current, remember we usually do one midyear in the edition life of the book. Send a self-addressed stamped #10 size envelope with "Snowbaby Update" written in the lower left corner to:

GREENBOOK
PO Box 645
Pacific Grove, CA   93950

As always, we welcome your comments and suggestions.

Thanks for buying the Guide.

Louise Langenfeld

Editor & Publisher

Note From The Publisher

Table of Contents

Table Of Contents

ARTCHARTS & LISTINGS

The GREENBOOK ARTCHARTS developed for the Department 56®️ Snowbabies™️ feature color photographs, factual information and TRUMARKET PRICES for each piece.

Factual information consists of Name, Item #, Introduction Date, Type of Product, Status, Material, Description and Item Particulars.

GREENBOOK TRUMARKET PRICE Listings include the Original Suggested Retail Price (OSRP), the current GREENBOOK TRUMARKET Secondary Market Price (GBTru), the percentage up or down as compared to the last edition of the Guide and the GBTru History Line.

A COMPLETE GUIDE

As a collectible grows, it becomes too difficult for the producer to create material which traces the history of the collection, detailing every nuance about every item. This is where the GREENBOOK becomes an invaluable tool for the collector. Each edition adds the new and the newly known. Everything is right at the collector's fingertips, in handy, easy-to-read formats.

GREENBOOK TRUMARKET PRICES

Secondary Market Prices are reported to us by retailers and collectors. The data is compiled, checked for accuracy, and a price established as a benchmark as a result of this research. There are many factors which determine the price a collector will pay for a piece; most acquisitions are a matter of personal judgement. The price will fluctuate with the time of year, section of the country and type of sale. GREENBOOK takes all of these factors into consideration when determining TRUMARKET Prices, and so **GREENBOOK TRUMARKET Prices are never an absolute number**. Use them as a basis for comparison, as a point of information when considering an acquisition, and as a guide when insuring for replacement value.

The GREENBOOK does not trade on the Secondary Market. The GREENBOOK monitors and reports prices, in the same way as the Wall Street Journal reports trades on the stock markets in the United States and abroad.

The GBTru History Line documents the Secondary Market History of each piece. Since 1991, we've published our Guides incorporating up-to-the-minute data in each new edition. The History line delineates Secondary Market history from 1991 to 1997. (There was no Guide published in calendar year 1996.)

What We Do

Throughout this edition of GREENBOOK are a variety of articles by Peter George, GREENBOOK's Department 56® Historian, that were previously printed in the Village Chronicle magazine. Though some of them appeared recently in the magazine and others are from issues dating back a year or more, the subject of each article is as valid now as when it was first published. We think you will enjoy reading these articles for their historical, informational and entertaining values.

Peter George is the publisher of the Village Chronicle magazine which he founded in 1991. Along with his publishing responsibilities, he also writes some of the articles and features for the magazine. Considered a Department 56® authority, he is a frequent guest speaker at gatherings and other Department 56® related events throughout the United States. As you might expect, one of his favorite pastimes is collecting Department 56® villages and Snowbabies™. This is Peter's fifth year as GREENBOOK's Department 56® Historian.

If you enjoy the articles from the Village Chronicle, subscribe to it today and continue the fun. Though each issue emphasizes the villages, there are entertaining and informative Snowbabies™ features as well. When you subscribe you'll receive page after page of:

- accurate, timely information and late-breaking news
- articles about each of the villages and Snowbabies™
- varied points of view from nationally recognized Department 56® authorities
- display advice & tips
- product highlights
- a calendar of Department 56® events
- classified ads so you can buy, sell, and trade
- and always much more

$24 for one year - 6 issues   (Canadian res: $29 US funds)
$44 for two years - 12 issues   (Canadian res: $49 US funds)
                                     R.I. residents add 7% sales tax.

Visa, MasterCard, Discover, American Express, Checks accepted

Subscribe by phone, fax, e-mail, mail, or visit our website.
  Phone: 401-467-9343
  Fax: 401-467-9359
  Website: http://www.villagechronicle.com
  E-mail: d56er@aol.com
  Mail: the Village Chronicle
    757 Park Ave.
    Cranston, RI 02910

Where Do Snowbabies™ Come From, Mommy?

Snowbabies™ are a quaint, little group of figurines including children, polar bears, penguins and other animals frolicking, playing, and always having fun. It's very easy to get caught up in the merriment of these snow-covered friends. Department 56, Inc. has produced these figurines since 1986, when many dealers were rather reluctant to sell them. Other retailers, however, realized that the Snowbabies™ would be a hit if given the chance.

The actual origin of Snowbabies™ dates from well before Department 56, Inc. began producing them, however. There are two theories as to where and how the figurines came into existence. One is that they were fashioned after Marie Ahnighito Peary, daughter of Admiral and Mrs. Peary, born September 12, 1893. Because she was the first baby with such light skin to be born in Greenland, the Eskimos named her Ah-Poo-Mackaninny (Snow Baby). Her middle name was in honor of the Eskimo woman who made her snowsuit.

At the turn of the century, Mrs. Peary authored books featuring The Snow Baby. They told of a child in the northlands. They were illustrated with drawings of the child, who was always depicted in a fluffy snowsuit, accompanied by animals that roamed the north. Marie went on to publish her own book in 1934, *The Snow Baby's Own Story*.

The other theory is based on a Christmas decoration that dates back to the early 1800's. A popular German candy doll called a Sugar Doll was said to have been the origin for the depiction of the first known Snowbaby bisque porcelain figurines. Produced in Germany in the early 1900's, many were shipped to the U.S. There is no evidence to offer concrete proof that these figurines were based on the Sugar Doll or Marie Peary's popularity, but it is agreed that the popularity of the Peary family, especially that of Admiral Peary, did lead to the Snowbabies™ becoming so sought after in this country.

Though present day collectors of Snowbabies™ may be interested in the origin of their collection, most are just thankful that Department 56, Inc. had the insight to produce them once again. And in large part, it has been artist Kristi Jensen Pierro and others at Department 56, Inc. who have continued to provide us with the happiness and carefree life that the Snowbabies™ represent.

the **Village Chronicle**.

SNOWBABIES™ FAQ
(Frequently Asked Questions)

1. After so many years without a company-sponsored collectors club of any kind, why did Department 56, Inc. decide to start one for the Snowbabies™?

   There are many reasons for a manufacturer to begin a collectors club. One is to create and/or maintain enthusiasm for the collectible. Another is to provide a benefit for collectors similar to that of a competitive product. In any case, it certainly adds another facet to the fun of collecting.

2. Who designs the Snowbabies™, and how do they come up with the various designs?

   Snowbabies™ are designed by a team of two creators, artist Kristi Jensen Pierro and Bill Kirchner–Department 56, Inc.'s Vice President of Product Development and Advertising. The two collaborate on all concepts and designs. Mr. Kirchner's baby picture was the original model for the face of the Snowbabies. Ms. Pierro uses children–her own and others–as subjects and models for her drawings. Mr. Kirchner has also been one of her models.

3. Are the Snowbabies™ male or female?

   They are neither. They simply represent playful children.

4. Will the little girl featured on the first Snowbabies Friendship Club™ Redemption Piece be used in many upcoming designs?

   Department 56, Inc. has stated that the little girl, the second human figure other than Snowbabies™ to grace the designs–Jack Frost was the first–will only appear in Snowbabies Friendship Club™ designs.

5. Is there a safe way to clean my Snowbabies™?

   Yes, but be careful. You don't want to remove any of the bisque "crystals" from the figures. One way to remove dust is to lightly brush it with a feather duster. Another is to blow away the dust with bursts from a can of compressed air. These cans are available at photographic and computer stores.

6. Why is the Snowbabies™ retirement day now different from that of the villages?

    It makes sense to separate the retirement day for Snowbabies™ so the collectible can have the opportunity to have its own special day instead of being overshadowed by the excitement that is generated by the retirement of the villages. This way Department 56, Inc., Snowbabies™ retailers, and Snowbabies™ collectors can concentrate on the little figurines.

7. Are Snowbunnies® the spring version of Snowbabies?™ What about the Easter animals?

     *It's obvious that the concept of the Snowbunnies® is derived directly from the Snowbabies™, and many Snowbabies™ collectors have adopted them into their collections. Though the inception of the Snowbunnies® allowed Department 56, Inc. to sell a similar product in the spring, they are two separate entities. The collectibility of one does not affect that of the other*

    The Easter Collectible animals are actually based upon a line of earlier Department 56® animals which had a smooth finish. The dated animals with "crystals" on them which first appeared in 1991 have also been adopted by many Snowbabies™ collectors.

8. Have there ever been any pins made to represent the Snowbabies™?

    Yes, there have been several Snowbabies™ pins manufactured by Department 56, Inc.:

     a. The first was actually a "snowflake" button that was distributed to collectors who attended the International Collectible Exposition in South Bend, Indiana in 1992.

    b. The "Noel" pin was given away to collectors at the Snowbabies™ open house event that took place at participating dealers in 1993.

     *c. "I'm Making Snowballs" was given to collectors who attended Department* 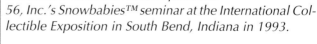 *56, Inc.'s Snowbabies™ seminar at the International Collectible Exposition in South Bend, Indiana in 1993.*

FAQ

d. The last pin to be distributed at an International Collectible Exposition was "Give Me A Push." This was given to collectors at the 1994 Expo in Secaucus, New Jersey.

e. The Snowbabies™ Friendship Pin was available at the December 1997 Snowbabies™ event.

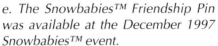

f. Similar to the Snowbabies™ Friendship Pin, the Snowbabies Friendship Club™ pin is available to collectors who join the Club. The Snowbabies™ are identical on both pins, but the club pin has a metal plaque attached that is designed to hold charms indicating years of membership in the Club.

9. Why did Department 56, Inc. begin making Snowbabies™ as glass ornaments?

    Glass ornaments have become a very popular collectible in the past few years. It would be safe to assume that Department 56, Inc. recognized the possibility that exists in this market and wanted to expand a current line into it. Likewise, collectors have the opportunity to collect Snowbabies™ in another medium.

10. Are the miniature pewter Snowbabies™ as collectible as their larger bisque cousins?

    Though many people do collect the mini Snowbabies™, they aren't as popular as the bisque ones. There may be a number of reasons for this including the size difference and that the bisque Snowbabies™ have more detail.

11. Will GREENBOOK publish software to keep track of the Snowbabies™ like it does for the villages?

    Yes, please see page 7 for more information.

FAQ

GREENBOOK'S
History List
of

Department 56® INC.

Snowbabies™

*1986-1997**

*Year of introduction indicates the year the piece was designed, sculpted and copyrighted. It is possible these pieces may not be available to the collector until the following calendar year.

Item #	Name	Intro		Retired
	SNOWBABIES™			
7950-2	Catch A Falling Star (Music Box)	1986		1987
7952-9	Snowbaby Sitting (Lite-up, Clip-on Ornament)	1986	✔	1990
7953-7	Snowbaby Crawling (Lite-up, Clip-on Ornament)	1986	✓	1992
7954-5	Snowbaby Winged (Lite-up, Clip-on Ornament)	1986		1990
7955-3	Give Me A Push!	1986		1990
7956-1	Hold On Tight!	1986		Current
7958-8	Best Friends	1986		1989
7959-6	Snowbaby Nite Lite	1986		1989
7961-8	Snowbaby On Brass Ribbon Ornament	1986		1989
7962-6	I'm Making Snowballs!	1986		1992
7963-4	Frosty Forest (Accessories)	1986		Current
7964-2	Snowbaby Standing (Waterglobe)	1986		1987
7965-0	Snowbaby Climbing On Snowball (Bisque votive w/candle)	1986		1989
7966-9	Snowbabies™ Hanging Pair (Figurines for votive, votive not included)	1986		1989
7967-7	Catch A Falling Star (Waterglobe, Music Box)	1986		1987
7970-7	Snowbaby Holding Picture Frame	1986		1987
7951-0	Moon Beams (Ornament)	1987		Current
7957-0	Tumbling In The Snow!	1987		1993
7960-0	Down The Hill We Go!	1987		Current
7968-5	Don't Fall Off!	1987		1990
7969-3	Snowbaby Adrift (Lite-up, Clip-on Ornament)	1987		1990
7971-5	Snowbabies™ Climbing On Tree	1987		1989
7972-3	Don't Fall Off! (Music Box)	1987		1993
7973-1	Snowbaby With Wings (Lighted Waterglobe)	1987		1988
7974-0	Winter Surprise!	1987		1992
7975-8	Snowbabies™ Riding Sleds (Jumbo Waterglobe, Music Box)	1987		1988
7976-6	Snowbaby-Mini, Winged Pair (Lite-up, Clip-on Ornament)	1987		Current
7730-5	Allison & Duncan (Dolls)	1988		1989
7977-4	Are All These Mine?	1988		Current
7978-2	Polar Express	1988	✔	1992
7979-0	Tiny Trio	1988		1990
7980-4	Twinkle Little Star (Ornament)	1988		1990
7981-2	Frosty Frolic	1988		Ltd Ed 4,800
7982-0	Helpful Friends	1989		1993
7983-9	Frosty Fun	1989		1991
7984-7	All Fall Down	1989		1991
7985-5	Finding Fallen Stars	1989		Ltd Ed 6,000
7986-3	Penguin Parade	1989		1992
7987-1	Icy Igloo w/Switch, Cord & Bulb (Accessory)	1989		Current
7988-0	Noel (Ornament)	1989		Current
7989-8	Surprise! (Ornament)	1989		1994
7990-1	Star Bright (Ornament)	1989	✔	Current
7992-8	Let It Snow (Waterglobe, Music Box)	1989		1993

Calendar History List

Item #	Name	Intro	Retired
7935-9	What Are You Doing? (Waterglobe, Music Box)	1990	Never Released
7937-5	All Tired Out (Waterglobe, Music Box)	1990	1992
7939-1	Rock-A-Bye Baby (Ornament)	1990	1995
7940-5	Penguin (Lite-up, Clip-on Ornament)	1990	1992
7941-3	Polar Bear (Lite-up, Clip-on Ornament)	1990	1992
7942-1	Twinkle Little Stars	1990	1993
7943-0	Wishing On A Star	1990	1994
7945-6	Read Me A Story!	1990	Current
7946-4	We Will Make It Shine!	1990	1992
7947-2	Playing Games Is Fun!	1990	1993
7948-0	A Special Delivery	1990	1994
7949-9	Who Are You?	1990	Ltd Ed 12,500
6800-4	I'll Put Up The Tree!	1991	1995
6801-2	Why Don't You Talk To Me?	1991	Current
6802-0	I Made This Just For You!	1991	Current
6803-9	Is That For Me?	1991	1993
6804-7	Polar Sign (Accessory)	1991	1996
6805-5	This Is Where We Live!	1991	1994
6807-1	Waiting For Christmas	1991	1993
6808-0	Dancing To A Tune	1991	1995
6809-8	Fishing For Dreams	1991	1994
6810-1	Swinging On A Star (Ornament)	1991	Current
6811-0	My First Star (Ornament)	1991	Current
7632-5	Playing Games Is Fun! (Revolving Music Box)	1991	1993
7633-3	Penguin Parade (Revolving Music Box)	1991	1994
7634-1	Frosty Frolic (2-Tier Music Box)	1991	1993
7635-0	Snowbabies™ Advent Tree W/24 Orns (Music Box)	1991	1994
7936-7	Play Me A Tune (Waterglobe, Music Box)	1991	1993
7938-3	Peek-A-Boo (Waterglobe, Music Box)	1991	1993
6806-3	Can I Help, Too?	1992	Ltd Ed 18,500
6812-8	Wait For Me!	1992	1994
6813-6	I Need A Hug	1992	Current
6814-4	Winken, Blinken, & Nod	1992	Current
6815-2	Let's Go Skiing	1992	Current
6816-0	This Will Cheer You Up	1992	1994
6817-9	Help Me, I'm Stuck!	1992	1994
6818-7	You Can't Find Me!	1992	1996
6819-5	Look What I Can Do!	1992	1996
6820-9	Shall I Play For You?	1992	Current
6821-7	You Didn't Forget Me!	1992	Current
6822-5	Stars-In-A-Row, Tic-Tac-Toe	1992	1995
6823-3	Just One Little Candle	1992	Current
6824-1	Join The Parade	1992	1994
6825-0	Snowbabies™ Icicle With Star (Ornaments)	1992	1995
6826-8	What Will I Catch? (Music Box)	1992	Current
6828-4	Over The Milky Way (Accessory)	1992	1995
6829-2	Starry Pines (Accessorries)	1992	Current
6830-6	Starry, Starry Night (Ornament)	1992	Current
6831-4	Read Me A Story! (Waterglobe, Music Box)	1992	1996
6832-2	Fishing For Dreams (Waterglobe, Music Box)	1992	1994

Calendar History List

Item #	Name	Intro	Retired
6833-0	Look What I Found!	1993	1997
6834-9	Crossing Starry Skies	1993	1997
6835-7	I'll Teach You A Trick	1993	1996
6836-5	I Found Your Mittens!	1993	1996
6837-3	So Much Work To Do!	1993	Current
6838-1	Can I Open It Now?	1993	Event Piece
6839-0	Now I Lay Me Down To Sleep	1993	Current
6840-3	Somewhere In Dreamland	1993	1997
6841-1	Where Did He Go?	1993	Current
6842-0	I'm Making An Ice Sculpture!	1993	1996
6843-8	We Make A Great Pair	1993	Current
6844-6	Will It Snow Today?	1993	1995
6845-4	Let's All Chime In!	1993	1995
6846-2	Baby's First Smile (Picture Frame)	1993	Current
6847-0	Wee ... This Is Fun! (Ornament)	1993	1997
6848-9	Sprinkling Stars In The Sky (Ornament)	1993	1997
6849-7	So Much Work To Do! (Waterglobe, Music Box)	1993	1995
6850-0	You Didn't Forget Me! (Waterglobe, Music Box)	1993	1997
6851-9	I'm So Sleepy (Revolving Music Box)	1993	Current
6857-8	Snowbabies™ Animated Book Music Box		
	(Music Box)	1993	1995
7646-5	Penguin Parade (Acrylic Music Box)	1993	1994
7647-3	Wishing On A Star (Acrylic Music Box)	1993	1994
7648-1	Can I Open It Now? (Acrylic Music Box)	1993	1994
7649-0	Reading A Story (Acrylic Music Box)	1993	1994
7650-3	Frosty Fun (Acrylic Music Box)	1993	1994
7651-1	Play Me A Tune (Acrylic Music Box)	1993	1994
714-5	Mickey's New Friend	1994	1995
6852-7	I'm Right Behind You!	1994	1997
6853-5	There's Another One!	1994	Current
6854-3	Jack Frost ... A Touch Of Winter's Magic	1994	Current
6855-1	Gathering Stars In The Sky (Ornament)	1994	1997
6856-0	Where Did You Come From?	1994	1997
6858-6	First Star Jinglebaby (Ornament)	1994	1997
6859-4	Little Drummer Jinglebaby (Ornament)	1994	1997
6860-8	Let's Go Skating	1994	Current
6861-6	Stringing Fallen Stars	1994	Current
6862-4	Bringing Starry Pines	1994	1997
6863-2	Lift Me Higher, I Can't Reach!	1994	Current
6864-0	Pennies From Heaven (Bank)	1994	Current
6865-9	We'll Plant The Starry Pines	1994	1997
6866-7	Be My Baby (Block Ornament)	1994	Current
6867-5	Juggling Stars In The Sky (Ornament)	1994	Current
6868-3	Stars In My Stocking Jinglebaby (Ornament)	1994	Current
6869-1	Just For You Jinglebaby (Ornament)	1994	Current
6870-5	Planting Starry Pines (Waterglobe, Music Box)	1994	1996
6871-3	Catch A Falling Star (Music Box)	1994	1997
6872-1	Look What I Found! (Waterglobe, Music Box)	1994	1997
6873-0	"Winter Tales Of The Snowbabies" (Book)	1994	Current

Calendar History List

Item #	Name	Intro	Retired
759-5	Overnight Delivery (Ornament)	1995	Event Piece
7800	"Star Gazing" Starter Set (Figurines/Accessories)	1995	1996
6874-8	I Found The Biggest Star Of All!	1995	Current
6875-6	Are You On My List?	1995	Current
6876-4	Ring The Bells ... It's Christmas!	1995	Current
6877-2	What Shall We Do Today?	1995	1997
6878-0	I See You!	1995	Current
6879-7	Are You On My List? (Waterglobe, Music Box)	1995	1997
68798	I'll Hug You Goodnight (Waterglobe, Music Box)	1995	Current
68799	Skate With Me (Waterglobe, Music Box)	1995	Current
68800	I Can't Find Him!	1995	Current
68801	I'll Play A Christmas Tune	1995	Current
68802	We're Building An Icy Igloo	1995	Current
68803	A Star-In-The-Box	1995	Event Piece
68804	Parade Of Penguins	1995	Current
68805	Mush!	1995	Current
68806	One Little Candle Jinglebaby (Ornament)	1995	Current
68807	Joy (Ornaments)	1995	Current
68808	Overnight Delivery (Ornament)	1995	Current
68809	Play Me A Tune (Music Box)	1995	Current
7668-6	Animated Skating Pond (Accessory)	1995	Current
76687	Frosty Pines (Accessories)	1995	Current
68810	I'm So Sleepy	1996	Current
68811	Jack Frost ... A Sleighride Through The Stars	1996	Current
68812	Which Way's Up?	1996	1997
68813	With Hugs & Kisses	1996	Current
68814	You Are My Lucky Star	1996	Current
68815	Once Upon A Time ... (Figurines/Votive Cup)	1996	Current
68816	Climb Every Mountain	1996	Ltd Ed 22,500
68817	Stargazing (Figurines/Accessories)	1996	Current
68818	You Need Wings Too!	1996	Current
68819	When The Bough Breaks	1996	Current
68820	There's No Place Like Home	1996	Current
68821	It's Snowing!	1996	Current
68822	It's A Grand Old Flag	1996	Current
68823	A Little Night Light	1996	Current
68824	Five-Part Harmony	1996	Current
68825	Starry Pine Jinglebaby (Ornament)	1996	Current
68826	Jinglebell Jinglebaby (Ornament)	1996	Current
68827	Snowbaby In My Stocking (Ornament)	1996	Current
68828	Baby's 1st Rattle (Ornament)	1996	Current
68829	Joy To The World (Ornament)	1996	Current
68830	Practice Makes Perfect (Waterglobe, Music Box)	1996	Current
68831	Now I Lay Me Down To Sleep (Waterglobe, Music Box)	1996	Current
68832	Once Upon A Time (Animated Moving Musical)	1996	Current
68833	Sliding Through The Milky Way (Music Box)	1996	Current
68834	You're My Snowbaby (Picture Frame)	1996	Current
68835	Moonbeams (Night Light)	1996	Current
68836	A Little Night Light (Lamp)	1996	Current

Calendar History List

Item #	Name	Intro		Retired
68837	Display Your Favorite Snowbaby (Lamp)	1996		Current
68838	Snowbaby Display Sled (Accessory)	1996		Current
68839	Wish Upon A Falling Star	1997		Current
68840	Two Little Babies On The Go!	1997		Current
68842	Best Little Star	1997		Current
68843	Wishing You A Merry Christmas!	1997		Current
68844	One, Two, High Button Shoe (Ornament)	1997		Current
68845	Three, Four, No Room For One More			
	(Ornament)	1997		Current
68846	Surprise (Hinged Box)	1997		Current
68847	Celebrate (Hinged Box)	1997		Current
68848	Rock-A-Bye Baby (Hinged Box)	1997	✓	Event Piece
68849	Snowbabies™ 1997 Bisque Friendship Pin (Pin)	1997		Event Piece
68850	Celebrating A Snowbabies™ Journey,			
	1987 - 1998 ... Let's Go See Jack Frost	1997		Event Piece
68853	Heigh-Ho, Heigh-Ho, To Frolic Land We Go!	1997		Current
68854	Whistle While You Work	1997		Current
68855	Jingle Bell	1997		Current
68856	Starlight Serenade	1997		Current
68857	Thank You	1997		Current
68858	One For You, One For Me	1997		Current
68859	Ship O' Dreams	1997		Current
68860	All We Need Is Love	1997		Event Piece
68861	Candlelight Trees (Accessories)	1997		Current
68862	I'm The Star Atop Your Tree! (Tree Topper)	1997		Current
68863	Candle Light ... Season Bright (Tree Topper)	1997		Current
68864	Candle Light ... Season Bright			
	(Clip-on Ornament)	1997		Current
68865	Five, Six, A Drum With Sticks (Ornament)	1997		Current
68867	I Love You (Hinged Box)	1997		Event Piece
68868	Sweet Dreams (Hinged Box)	1997		Current
68869	Polar Express (Hinged Box)	1997		Current
68870	Did He See You? (Moving Musical Figurine)	1997	✓	Current
68871	Jingle Bell (Waterglobe, Music Box)	1997		Current
68872	Heigh-Ho (Waterglobe, Music Box)	1997		Current
68873	Moon Beams (Waterglobe, Music Box)	1997		Current
68874	Snowbabies™ Shelf Unit (Accessory)	1997		Current

SNOWBABIES™ MINIATURES

Item #	Name	Intro		Retired
7600-7	Hold On Tight!	1989		Current
7601-5	Give Me A Push!	1989		1994
7602-3	I'm Making Snowballs!	1989		Current
7603-1	Don't Fall Off!	1989		1994
7604-0	Best Friends	1989		1994
7605-8	Are All These Mine?	1989		1992
7606-6	Down The Hill We Go!	1989	✓	Current
7607-4	Winter Surprise!	1989	✓	1994
7608-2	Helpful Friends	1989		1992
7609-0	Polar Express	1989		1992
7610-4	Icy Igloo W/Tree	1989		1992
7611-2	Frosty Fun	1989		1997

Calendar History List

Item #	Name	Intro	Retired
7612-0	Frosty Forest	1989	Current
7613-9	Frosty Frolic	1989	1993
7614-7	Tumbling In The Snow!	1989	1992
7615-5	Tiny Trio	1989	1993
7616-3	Penguin Parade	1989	1993
7617-1	All Fall Down	1989	1993
7618-0	Finding Fallen Stars	1989	1992
7619-8	Frosty Frolic Land	1989	Current
7620-1	Collector's Sign	1989	Current
7621-0	Twinkle Little Stars	1990	1993
7622-8	Read Me A Story!	1990	1997
7623-6	Playing Games Is Fun!	1990	1993
7624-4	A Special Delivery	1990	1993
7625-2	Why Don't You Talk To Me?	1991	Current
7626-0	Wishing On A Star	1991	1995
7627-9	I'll Put Up The Tree!	1991	1996
7628-7	I Made This Just For You!	1991	1994
7629-5	Waiting For Christmas	1991	1993
7630-9	Dancing To A Tune	1991	1993
7631-7	Is That For Me?	1991	1993
7636-8	Let's Go Skiing	1992	Current
7637-6	You Can't Find Me!	1992	1996
7638-4	Help Me, I'm Stuck!	1992	1997
7639-2	This Will Cheer You Up	1992	1995
7640-6	I Need A Hug	1992	1997
7641-4	Wait For Me!	1992	1995
7642-2	Shall I Play For You?	1992	Current
7643-0	You Didn't Forget Me!	1992	1995
7644-9	Just One Little Candle	1992	Current
7645-7	Join The Parade	1992	1995
7652-0	We Make A Great Pair	1993	1997
7653-8	Will It Snow Today?	1993	Current
7654-6	Where Did He Go?	1993	Current
7655-4	Let's All Chime In!	1993	Current
7656-2	Somewhere In Dreamland	1993	1997
7657-0	Now I Lay Me Down To Sleep	1993	Current
7658-9	Winken, Blinken, & Nod	1993	Current
7661-9	There's Another One	1994	1997
7662-7	I'm Right Behind You	1994	1997
7663-5	We'll Plant The Starry Pines	1994	1997
7664-3	Let's Go Skating	1994	Current
7665-1	Stringing Fallen Stars	1994	Current
7666-0	Bringing Starry Pines	1994	1997
7667-8	Lift Me Higher, I Can't Reach!	1994	1997
76690	I Found The Biggest Star Of All	1995	Current
76691	Are You On My List?	1995	1997
76692	Ring The Bells ... It's Christmas!	1995	Current
76693	What Shall We Do Today?	1995	Current
76694	I See You!	1995	Current

Calendar History List

Item #	Name	Intro	Retired
76695	I Can't Find Him!	1995	Current
76696	I'll Play A Christmas Tune	1995	Current
76697	We're Building An Icy Igloo	1995	Current
76698	A Star-In-The-Box	1995	Current
76699	Mush!	1995	Current
76700	I'm So Sleepy	1996	Current
76701	Which Way's Up?	1996	Current
76702	Climb Every Mountain	1996	Current
76703	You Are My Lucky Star	1996	Current
76704	With Hugs & Kisses	1996	Current
76705	It's A Grand Old Flag	1996	Current
76706	It's Snowing!	1996	Current
76707	When The Bough Breaks	1996	Current
76708	There's No Place Like Home	1996	Current
76709	You Need Wings Too!	1996	Current
76710	Five-Part Harmony	1996	Current
76711	Heigh-Ho, Heigh-Ho, To Frolic Land We Go!	1997	Current
76712	Whistle While You Work	1997	Current
76713	Jingle Bell	1997	Current
76714	Starlight Serenade	1997	Current
76715	Thank You	1997	Current
76716	Jack Frost ... A Touch Of Winter's Magic	1997	Current
76717	Wish Upon A Falling Star	1997	Current
76718	Best Little Star	1997	Current
SNOWBABIES™ MERCURY GLASS			
68980	Snowbaby With Wreath	1996	Current
68981	Snowbaby On Package	1996	Current
68982	Snowbaby Soldier	1996	Current
68983	Snowbaby Drummer	1996	Current
68984	Snowbaby On Snowball	1996	Current
68986	Snowbaby In Package	1996	Current
68987	Snowbaby With Bell	1996	Current
68988	Snowbaby On Moon	1996	Current
68989	Snowbaby Jinglebaby	1996	Current
68990	Snowbaby With Tree	1996	Current
68991	Snowbaby With Star	1996	Current
68992	Snowbaby On Tree	1997	Current
68993	Snowbaby On Drum	1997	Current
68994	Snowbaby In Stocking	1997	Current
68995	Snowbaby On Skis	1997	Current
68996	Snowbaby In Skate	1997	Current
68997	Snowbaby Angel	1997	Current
68998	Snowbaby Jack Frost	1997	Current
SNOWBABIES FRIENDSHIP CLUB™			
68851	Friendship Club Membership Kit (includes "You Better Watch Out" Fig.)	1997	Member Only– Welcome Gift
68852	Together We Can Make The Season Bright	1997	Member Only– Redemption Piece

Retired

(continued)

Snowbabies™ QuikReference

Retired (continued)

Retired *(continued)*

ITEM #	RETIRED		
7970-7	1987	Snowbaby Holding Picture Frame	Picture Frames
7971-5	1989	Snowbabies™ Climbing On Tree	Figurines
7972-3	1993	Don't Fall Off!	Music Box
7973-1	1988	Snowbaby With Wings	Lighted Waterglobe
7974-0	1992 ✔	Winter Surprise!	Figurine
7975-8	1988	Snowbabies™ Riding Sleds	Jumbo Waterglobe, Music Box
7978-2	1992	Polar Express	Figurine
7979-0	1990 ✔	Tiny Trio	Figurines
7980-4	1990	Twinkle Little Star	Ornament
7982-0	1993	Helpful Friends	Figurine
7983-9	1991	Frosty Fun	Figurine
7984-7	1991	All Fall Down	Figurines
7986-3	1992	Penguin Parade	Figurine
7989-8	1994	Surprise!	Ornament
7992-8	1993	Let It Snow	Waterglobe, Music Box

Limited Editions

ITEM #	PIECES		
6806-3	18,500	Can I Help, Too?	Figurine
7949-9	12,500	Who Are You?	Figurine
7981-2	4,800	Frosty Frolic	Figurine
7985-5	6,000	Finding Fallen Stars	Figurine
68816	22,500	Climb Every Mountain	Figurine

Event Pieces

ITEM #	YEAR		
6838-1	1993	Can I Open It Now?	Figurine
759-5	1995	Overnight Delivery	Ornament
68803	1995	A Star-In-The-Box	Figurine
68848	1997	Rock-A-Bye Baby	✔ Hinged Box, Dated
68849	1997	Snowbabies™ 1997 Bisque Friendship Pin	Pin
68850	1997	Celebrating A Snowbabies™ Journey, 1987 - 1998 ... Let's Go See Jack Frost	Figurine
68860	1997	All We Need Is Love	Figurine
68867	1997	I Love You	Hinged Box

Snowbabies™ QuikReference

CATCH A FALLING STAR

ITEM #	INTRO	STATUS	OSRP	GBTRU	↑
7950-2	1986	RETIRED 1987	$27.50	**$695.00**	9%

Product: Music Box
Material: Porcelain
Description: Seated Snowbaby with outstretched arms.
Particulars: Tune: "Catch A Falling Star." Size is 7".

DATE:_____ $:_____		'91	'92	'93	'94	'95	'97
○ WISH ○ HAVE		$875	750	525	545	550	635

SNOWBABY SITTING

ITEM #	INTRO	STATUS	OSRP	GBTRU	↓
7952-9	1986	RETIRED 1990	$7.00	**$38.00**	14%

Product: Lite-up, Clip-on Ornament
Material: Porcelain
Description: Snowbaby sitting with open arms.
Particulars: May be lighted by placing a miniature Christmas light into opening. Size is 2.75".

DATE:_____ $:_____		'91	'92	'93	'94	'95	'97
○ WISH ◉ HAVE		$25	32	30	36	40	44

SNOWBABY CRAWLING

ITEM #	INTRO	STATUS	OSRP	GBTRU	↓
7953-7	1986	RETIRED 1992	$7.00	**$22.00**	12%

Product: Lite-up, Clip-on Ornament
Material: Porcelain
Description: Snowbaby crawling.
Particulars: May be lighted by placing a miniature Christmas light into opening. Size is 3.75".

DATE:_____ $:_____		'91	'92	'93	'94	'95	'97
○ WISH ◉ HAVE		$7.5	7.5	18	20	20	25

SNOWBABY WINGED

ITEM #	INTRO	STATUS	OSRP	GBTRU	↑
7954-5	1986	RETIRED 1990	$7.00	**$50.00**	11%

Product: Lite-up, Clip-on Ornament
Material: Porcelain
Description: Winged Snowbaby sitting with open arms.
Particulars: May be lighted by placing a miniature Christmas light into opening. Size is 2.75".

DATE:_____ $:_____		'91	'92	'93	'94	'95	'97
○ WISH ◉ HAVE		$25	35	35	38	45	45

Snowbabies™

Give Me A Push!

Item #	Intro	Status	OSRP	GBTru	↓
7955-3	1986	Retired 1990	$12.00	**$60.00**	8%

Product: Figurine
Material: Porcelain
Description: Snowbaby with open arms seated on sled.
Particulars: Size is 3.25".

DATE:	$:	'91	'92	'93	'94	'95	'97
○ WISH	○ HAVE	$30	35	42	54	60	65

Hold On Tight!

Item #	Intro	Status	OSRP	GBTru	NO
7956-1	1986	Current	$12.00	**$13.50**	CHANGE

Product: Figurine
Material: Porcelain
Description: Snowbaby lying on a sled.
Particulars: Size is 3.25"

DATE:	$:	'91	'92	'93	'94	'95	'97
○ WISH	○ HAVE	$13.5	13.5	13.5	13.5	13.5	13.5

Best Friends

Item #	Intro	Status	OSRP	GBTru	↓
7958-8	1986	Retired 1989	$12.00	**$105.00**	13%

Product: Figurine
Material: Porcelain
Description: Snowbabies™ put arms around each other.
Particulars: Size is 3.75".

DATE:	$:	'91	'92	'93	'94	'95	'97
○ WISH	○ HAVE	$70	75	116	118	120	120

Snowbaby Nite Lite

Item #	Intro	Status	OSRP	GBTru	↑
7959-6	1986	Retired 1989	$15.00	**$335.00**	2%

Product: Nite Lite
Material: Porcelain
Description: Snowbaby sitting with open arms.
Particulars: Plugs directly into electrical outlet. Size is 5.75".

DATE:	$:	'91	'92	'93	'94	'95	'97
○ WISH	○ HAVE	$285	285	265	230	275	330

Snowbabies™

SNOWBABY ON BRASS RIBBON ORNAMENT

ITEM #	INTRO	STATUS	OSRP	GBTRU	↓
7961-8	1986	RETIRED 1989	$8.00	**$150.00**	6%

Product: Ornament
Material: Porcelain
Description: Snowbaby on brass ribbon ornament.
Particulars: Size is 7.5".

DATE:_____ $:_____	'91	'92	'93	'94	'95	'97
○ WISH ○ HAVE	$50	65	95	112	125	160

I'M MAKING SNOWBALLS!

ITEM #	INTRO	STATUS	OSRP	GBTRU	↑
7962-6	1986	RETIRED 1992	$12.00	**$35.00**	17%

Product: Figurine
Material: Porcelain
Description: Snowbaby pushing giant snowball.
Particulars: Size is 3.25".

DATE:_____ $:_____	'91	'92	'93	'94	'95	'97
○ WISH ◉ HAVE	$13	13.5	30	30	30	30

FROSTY FOREST

ITEM #	INTRO	STATUS	OSRP	GBTRU	NO
7963-4	1986	CURRENT	$15.00	**$20.00**	CHANGE

Product: Accessories
Material: Porcelain
Description: Two snow covered trees.
Particulars: Set of 2. Sizes are 5" and 6".

DATE:_____ $:_____	'91	'92	'93	'94	'95	'97
○ WISH ○ HAVE	$20	20	20	20	20	20

SNOWBABY STANDING

ITEM #	INTRO	STATUS	OSRP	GBTRU	NO
7964-2	1986	RETIRED 1987	$7.50	**$425.00**	CHANGE

Product: Waterglobe
Material: Bisque/Glass/Resin
Description: Snowbaby standing.
Particulars: Size is 4.5".

DATE:_____ $:_____	'91	'92	'93	'94	'95	'97
○ WISH ○ HAVE	$NE	NE	NE	400	425	425

Snowbabies™

SNOWBABY CLIMBING ON SNOWBALL

ITEM #	INTRO	STATUS	OSRP	GBTRU	↓
7965-0	1986	RETIRED 1989	$15.00	**$105.00**	9%

Product: Bisque votive w/candle
Material: Porcelain
Description: Snowbaby climbing on snowball.
Particulars: Set of 2. Size is 3.75".

DATE:_____	$:_____	'91	'92	'93	'94	'95	'97
○ WISH	○ HAVE	$65	65	65	65	95	115

SNOWBABIES™ HANGING PAIR

ITEM #	INTRO	STATUS	OSRP	GBTRU	↓
7966-9	1986	RETIRED 1989	$15.00	**$145.00**	12%

Product: Figurines for votive, votive not included
Material: Porcelain
Description: Snowbabies™ pair.
Particulars: Set of 2. Size is 3.5".

DATE:_____	$:_____	'91	'92	'93	'94	'95	'97
○ WISH	○ HAVE	$70	70	100	140	160	165

CATCH A FALLING STAR

ITEM #	INTRO	STATUS	OSRP	GBTRU	↑
7967-7	1986	RETIRED 1987	$18.00	**$575.00**	1%

Product: Waterglobe, Music Box
Material: Bisque/Glass/Resin
Description: Seated Snowbaby with outstretched arms.
Particulars: Tune: "Catch A Falling Star." Size is 4.5".
    Variation: In color–white base instead of green.

DATE:_____	$:_____	'91	'92	'93	'94	'95	'97
○ WISH	○ HAVE	$NE	NE	NE	550	550	570

SNOWBABY HOLDING PICTURE FRAME

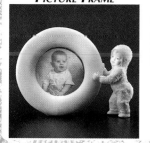

ITEM #	INTRO	STATUS	OSRP	GBTRU	↓
7970-7	1986	RETIRED 1987	$15.00	**$495.00**	12%

Product: Picture Frame
Material: Porcelain
Description: Snowbaby holding picture frame.
Particulars: Set of 2. Size is 4.75".

DATE:_____	$:_____	'91	'92	'93	'94	'95	'97
○ WISH	○ HAVE	$225	225	375	550	550	565

Snowbabies™

MOON BEAMS

ITEM #	INTRO	STATUS	OSRP	GBTRU	NO
7951-0	1987	CURRENT	$7.50	**$8.50**	CHANGE

Product: Ornament
Material: Porcelain
Description: Snowbaby sits on crescent moon.
Particulars: Size is 3.75".

DATE:	$:	'91	'92	'93	'94	'95	'97
○ WISH ● HAVE		$8.5	8.5	8.5	8.5	8.5	8.5

TUMBLING IN THE SNOW!

ITEM #	INTRO	STATUS	OSRP	GBTRU	NO
7957-0	1987	RETIRED 1993	$35.00	**$85.00**	CHANGE

Product: Figurines
Material: Porcelain
Description: Snowbabies™ tumbling.
Particulars: Set of 5. Sizes range from 2" to 3.25".

DATE:	$:	'91	'92	'93	'94	'95	'97
○ WISH ○ HAVE		$37.5	40	40	70	65	85

DOWN THE HILL WE GO!

ITEM #	INTRO	STATUS	OSRP	GBTRU	NO
7960-0	1987	CURRENT	$20.00	**$22.50**	CHANGE

Product: Figurine
Material: Porcelain
Description: Two Snowbabies™ on a toboggan.
Particulars: Size is 2.75".

DATE:	$:	'91	'92	'93	'94	'95	'97
○ WISH ● HAVE		$22	22.5	22.5	22.5	22.5	22.5

DON'T FALL OFF!

ITEM #	INTRO	STATUS	OSRP	GBTRU	↓
7968-5	1987	RETIRED 1990	$12.50	**$90.00**	5%

Product: Figurine
Material: Porcelain
Description: Snowbaby sitting on a snowball.
Particulars: Size is 5.5".

DATE:	$:	'91	'92	'93	'94	'95	'97
○ WISH ○ HAVE		$35	45	52	62	80	95

Snowbabies™

SNOWBABY ADRIFT

ITEM #	INTRO	STATUS	OSRP	GBTRU	↑
7969-3	1987	RETIRED 1990	$8.50	**$130.00**	4%

Product: Lite-up, Clip-on Ornament
Material: Porcelain
Description: Snowbaby on a snowflake.
Particulars: May be lighted by placing a miniature Christmas light into opening.

DATE:_____	$:_____	'91	'92	'93	'94	'95	'97
○ WISH	○ HAVE	$25	45	55	92	120	125

SNOWBABIES™ CLIMBING ON TREE

ITEM #	INTRO	STATUS	OSRP	GBTRU	↓
7971-5	1987	RETIRED 1989	$25.00	**$855.00**	2%

Product: Figurines
Material: Porcelain
Description: One Snowbaby watches another climbing tree.
Particulars: Set of 2. Size is 8". The Snowbaby on top of tree is separate.

DATE:_____	$:_____	'91	'92	'93	'94	'95	'97
○ WISH	○ HAVE	$NE	425	450	535	750	870

DON'T FALL OFF!

ITEM #	INTRO	STATUS	OSRP	GBTRU	↑
7972-3	1987	RETIRED 1993	$30.00	**$52.00**	4%

Product: Music Box
Material: Porcelain
Description: Snowbaby sitting on snowball.
Particulars: Tune: "When You Wish Upon A Star." Size is 6.5".

DATE:_____	$:_____	'91	'92	'93	'94	'95	'97
○ WISH	○ HAVE	$32	35	35	45	40	50

SNOWBABY WITH WINGS

ITEM #	INTRO	STATUS	OSRP	GBTRU	NO
7973-1	1987	RETIRED 1988	$20.00	**$425.00**	CHANGE

Product: Lighted Waterglobe
Material: Bisque/Glass/Resin
Description: Snowbaby sits with outstretched arms
Particulars: Lighted by batteries. Size is 5.5".

DATE:_____	$:_____	'91	'92	'93	'94	'95	'97
○ WISH	○ HAVE	$NE	385	385	385	395	425

Snowbabies™

WINTER SURPRISE!

ITEM #	INTRO	STATUS	OSRP	GBTRU	↓
7974-0	1987	RETIRED 1992	$15.00	**$35.00**	8%

Product: Figurine
Material: Porcelain
Description: Two Snowbabies™ peek out of gift box.
Particulars: Size is 3".

DATE:	$:	'91	'92	'93	'94	'95	'97
○ WISH	◉ HAVE	$17.5	17.5	35	35	35	38

SNOWBABIES™ RIDING SLEDS

ITEM #	INTRO	STATUS	OSRP	GBTRU	↑
7975-8	1987	RETIRED 1988	$40.00	**$800.00**	3%

Product: Jumbo Waterglobe, Music Box
Material: Bisque/Glass/Resin
Description: Snowbabies™ sled down hill between evergreen trees.
Particulars: Tune: "Winter Wonderland." Size is 7.25".

DATE:	$:	'91	'92	'93	'94	'95	'97
○ WISH	○ HAVE	$NE	NE	NE	650	650	780

SNOWBABY-MINI, WINGED PAIR

ITEM #	INTRO	STATUS	OSRP	GBTRU	NO
7976-6	1987	CURRENT	$9.00	**$12.00**	CHANGE

Product: Lite-up, Clip-on Ornament
Material: Porcelain
Description: Seated Snowbaby with open arms.
Particulars: Package of 2. May be lighted by placing a miniature Christmas light into opening. Size is 2.25".

DATE:	$:	'91	'92	'93	'94	'95	'97
○ WISH	◉ HAVE	$11	12	12	12	12	12

ALLISON & DUNCAN

ITEM #	INTRO	STATUS	OSRP	GBTRU	↑
7730-5	1988	RETIRED 1989	$200.00	**$1125.00**	45%

Product: Dolls
Material: Papier-mâché
Description: Snowbaby boy and girl dolls dressed for frigid wintry weather. High laced boots, feathery trim on coats, hats, and pants.
Particulars: Set of 2.

DATE:	$:	'91	'92	'93	'94	'95	'97
○ WISH	○ HAVE	$ -	750	700	700	700	775

Snowbabies™

ARE ALL THESE MINE?

ITEM #	INTRO	STATUS	OSRP	GBTru	NO
7977-4	1988	CURRENT	$10.00	**$12.50**	CHANGE

Product: Figurine
Material: Porcelain
Description: Snowbaby holds stocking full of stars.
Particulars: Size is 3.5".

DATE:_____ $:_____	'91	'92	'93	'94	'95	'97
○ WISH ● HAVE	$12	12.5	12.5	12.5	12.5	12.5

POLAR EXPRESS

ITEM #	INTRO	STATUS	OSRP	GBTru	↓
7978-2	1988	RETIRED 1992	$22.00	**$85.00**	12%

Product: Figurine
Material: Porcelain
Description: Two Snowbabies™ ride a polar bear.
Particulars: Size is 5.75".

DATE:_____ $:_____	'91	'92	'93	'94	'95	'97
○ WISH ● HAVE	$30	32.5	55	55	55	97

TINY TRIO

ITEM #	INTRO	STATUS	OSRP	GBTru	↓
7979-0	1988	RETIRED 1990	$20.00	**$155.00**	11%

Product: Figurines
Material: Porcelain
Description: Snowbaby band.
Particulars: Set of 3. Size is 3.5".

DATE:_____ $:_____	'91	'92	'93	'94	'95	'97
○ WISH ● HAVE	$70	75	90	102	145	175

TWINKLE LITTLE STAR

ITEM #	INTRO	STATUS	OSRP	GBTru	NO
7980-4	1988	RETIRED 1990	$7.00	**$80.00**	CHANGE

Product: Ornament
Material: Porcelain
Description: Snowbaby as a star.
Particulars: Size is 5".

DATE:_____ $:_____	'91	'92	'93	'94	'95	'97
○ WISH ○ HAVE	$25	30	32	82	80	80

Snowbabies™

Frosty Frolic

Item #	Intro	Status	OSRP	GBTru	↓
7981-2	1988	Ltd Ed 4,800	$35.00	**$965.00**	3%

Product: Figurine
Material: Porcelain
Description: Snowbabies™ hold hands and circle tree.
Particulars: Size is 5".

DATE:_____ $:_____	'91	'92	'93	'94	'95	'97
○ WISH ○ HAVE	$575	715	715	785	795	990

Helpful Friends

Item #	Intro	Status	OSRP	GBTru	NO
7982-0	1989	Retired 1993	$30.00	**$45.00**	CHANGE

Product: Figurine
Material: Porcelain
Description: Snowbaby and penguins with box of stars.
Particulars: Size is 6".

DATE:_____ $:_____	'91	'92	'93	'94	'95	'97
○ WISH ○ HAVE	$32.5	34	34	55	55	45

Frosty Fun

Item #	Intro	Status	OSRP	GBTru	↓
7983-9	1989	Retired 1991	$27.50	**$50.00**	9%

Product: Figurine
Material: Porcelain
Description: Snowbabies™ building a snowman.
Particulars: Size is 4".

DATE:_____ $:_____	'91	'92	'93	'94	'95	'97
○ WISH ○ HAVE	$30	50	75	55	55	55

All Fall Down

Item #	Intro	Status	OSRP	GBTru	↓
7984-7	1989	Retired 1991	$36.00	**$55.00**	8%

Product: Figurines
Material: Porcelain
Description: Ice-skating Snowbabies™ fall down.
Particulars: Set of 4. Size is 4.25".

DATE:_____ $:_____	'91	'92	'93	'94	'95	'97
○ WISH ○ HAVE	$40	55	72	60	60	60

Snowbabies™

The Snowbabies™ Top Ten

Snowbabies™ are not often mentioned in conversations about the secondary market. Sure, it is fairly easy to find out how much each piece is selling for; just look it up in any broker's listing. But do you know which Snowbaby has the highest value? O.K., so you got that one right. It was pretty easy. But what is the fourth highest…or the seventh? And which are sold most often?

Top 10
Snowbabies™ with the
Highest Secondary Value

10. Snowbaby With Wings
9. Snowbaby Standing
8. Snowbabies™ Holding Picture Frame
7. Catch A Falling Star
6. Mickey's New Friend
5. Catch A Falling Star
4. Snowbabies™ Riding Sleds
3. Snowbabies™ Climbing On Tree
2. Frosty Frolic

and the **Number One** Snowbaby with the highest secondary value…
Allison & Duncan

Top 10
Best Selling Snowbabies™

10. I'm Making Snowballs!
9. Who Are You?
8. All Fall Down
7. Winter Surprise!
6. Don't Fall Off!
5. Mickey's New Friend
4. Snowbaby Adrift
3. Best Friends
2. Tiny Trio ✓

and the **Number One** best-selling Snowbaby…
Tumbling In The Snow!

the **Village Chronicle**.

Snowbabies™

FINDING FALLEN STARS

ITEM #	INTRO	STATUS	OSRP	GBTRU	↓
7985-5	1989	LTD ED 6,000	$32.50	**$145.00**	12%

Product: Figurine
Material: Porcelain
Description: Snowbabies™ collect fallen stars in basket.
Particulars: Size is 6".

DATE:_____ $:_____	'91	'92	'93	'94	'95	'97
○ WISH ○ HAVE	$145	135	175	165	165	165

PENGUIN PARADE

ITEM #	INTRO	STATUS	OSRP	GBTRU	↓
7986-3	1989	RETIRED 1992	$25.00	**$45.00**	18%

Product: Figurine
Material: Porcelain
Description: Penguins follow Snowbaby playing flute.
Particulars: Size is 5".

DATE:_____ $:_____	'91	'92	'93	'94	'95	'97
○ WISH ○ HAVE	$27.5	30	36	52	50	55

ICY IGLOO W/SWITCH, CORD & BULB

ITEM #	INTRO	STATUS	OSRP	GBTRU	
7987-1	1989	CURRENT	$37.50	**$37.50**	NO CHANGE

Product: Accessory
Material: Porcelain
Description: Snow house.
Particulars: Lighted. Size is 7.5".

DATE:_____ $:_____	'91	'92	'93	'94	'95	'97
○ WISH ○ HAVE	$37.5	37.5	37.5	37.5	37.5	37.5

NOEL

ITEM #	INTRO	STATUS	OSRP	GBTRU	
7988-0	1989	CURRENT	$7.50	**$7.50**	NO CHANGE

Product: Ornament
Material: Porcelain
Description: Flying Snowbaby plays horn.
Particulars: Size is 4.5".

DATE:_____ $:_____	'91	'92	'93	'94	'95	'97
○ WISH ○ HAVE	$7.5	7.5	7.5	7.5	7.5	7.5

Snowbabies™

SURPRISE!

ITEM #	INTRO	STATUS	OSRP	GBTRU	↓
7989-8	1989	RETIRED 1994	$12.00	**$24.00**	14%

Product: Ornament
Material: Porcelain
Description: Snowbaby peeks out of gift box.
Particulars: Size is 3".

DATE:_____	$:_____	'91	'92	'93	'94	'95	'97
○ WISH	○ HAVE	$12	12	12	12	27	28

STAR BRIGHT

ITEM #	INTRO	STATUS	OSRP	GBTRU	NO
7990-1	1989	CURRENT	$7.50	**$7.50**	CHANGE

Product: Ornament
Material: Porcelain
Description: Snowbaby climbs on a star.
Particulars: Size is 4".

DATE:_____	$:_____	'91	'92	'93	'94	'95	'97
○ WISH	● HAVE	$7.5	7.5	7.5	7.5	7.5	7.5

LET IT SNOW

ITEM #	INTRO	STATUS	OSRP	GBTRU	↑
7992-8	1989	RETIRED 1993	$25.00	**$55.00**	10%

Product: Waterglobe, Music Box
Material: Bisque/Glass/Resin
Description: Snowbabies™ ride on polar bear.
Particulars: Tune: "Winter Wonderland." Size is 4".

DATE:_____	$:_____	'91	'92	'93	'94	'95	'97
○ WISH	○ HAVE	$25	27.5	27.5	35	40	50

WHAT ARE YOU DOING?

ITEM #	INTRO	STATUS
7935-9	1990	NEVER RELEASED

Product: Waterglobe, Music Box
Material: Bisque/Glass/Resin

Particulars: Tune: "Twinkle, Twinkle, Little Star." Never released due to production problems. The penguins outside globe were too fragile.

DATE:_____ $:_____
○ WISH   ○ HAVE

Snowbabies™

ALL TIRED OUT

Item #	Intro	Status	OSRP	GBTru	↓
7937-5	1990	Retired 1992	$55.00	**$60.00**	8%

Product: Waterglobe, Music Box
Material: Bisque/Glass/Resin
Description: Snowbaby takes a nap.
Particulars: Tune: "Brahms' Lullaby." Size is 7".

DATE:	$:		'91	'92	'93	'94	'95	'97
○ WISH	○ HAVE		$55	55	68	68	60	65

ROCK-A-BYE BABY

Item #	Intro	Status	OSRP	GBTru	↑
7939-1	1990	Retired 1995	$7.00	**$15.00**	25%

Product: Ornament
Material: Porcelain
Description: Snowbaby naps on crescent moon with garland of stars.
Particulars: Size is 3.5".

DATE:	$:		'91	'92	'93	'94	'95	'97
○ WISH	⦿ HAVE		$7	7	7.5	7.5	7.5	12

PENGUIN

Item #	Intro	Status	OSRP	GBTru	↓
7940-5	1990	Retired 1992	$5.00	**$22.00**	8%

Product: Lite-up, Clip-on Ornament
Material: Porcelain
Description: Penguin.
Particulars: May be lighted by placing a miniature Christmas light into opening. Size is 3".

DATE:	$:		'91	'92	'93	'94	'95	'97
○ WISH	○ HAVE		$5	5	15	15	15	24

POLAR BEAR

Item #	Intro	Status	OSRP	GBTru	↓
7941-3	1990	Retired 1992	$5.00	**$18.00**	10%

Product: Lite-up, Clip-on Ornament
Material: Porcelain
Description: Polar Bear.
Particulars: May be lighted by placing a miniature Christmas light into opening. Size is 3.5".

DATE:	$:		'91	'92	'93	'94	'95	'97
○ WISH	○ HAVE		$5	5	12	18	20	20

Snowbabies™

TWINKLE LITTLE STARS

ITEM #	INTRO	STATUS	OSRP	GBTRU	↓
7942-1	1990	RETIRED 1993	$37.50	**$50.00**	9%

Product: Figurines
Material: Porcelain
Description: Three Snowbabies™ sing carols.
Particulars: Set of 2. Size is 4".

DATE:_____	$:_____	'91	'92	'93	'94	'95	'97
○ WISH	○ HAVE	$37.5	37.5	40	55	45	55

WISHING ON A STAR

ITEM #	INTRO	STATUS	OSRP	GBTRU	↓
7943-0	1990	RETIRED 1994	$20.00	**$40.00**	11%

Product: Figurine
Material: Porcelain
Description: Penguin watches Snowbaby holding up star to wish upon.
Particulars: Size is 3.5".

DATE:_____	$:_____	'91	'92	'93	'94	'95	'97
○ WISH	○ HAVE	$20	21	22	22	42	45

READ ME A STORY!

ITEM #	INTRO	STATUS	OSRP	GBTRU	
7945-6	1990	CURRENT	$25.00	**$25.00**	NO CHANGE

Product: Figurine
Material: Porcelain
Description: Snowbaby reads story to penguins.
Particulars: Size is 3.5".

DATE:_____	$:_____	'91	'92	'93	'94	'95	'97
○ WISH	○ HAVE	$25	25	25	25	25	25

WE WILL MAKE IT SHINE!

ITEM #	INTRO	STATUS	OSRP	GBTRU	↓
7946-4	1990	RETIRED 1992	$45.00	**$58.00**	23%

Product: Figurine
Material: Porcelain
Description: Snowbabies™ hang stars on tree.
Particulars: Size is 7.5".

DATE:_____	$:_____	'91	'92	'93	'94	'95	'97
○ WISH	○ HAVE	$45	48	85	80	75	75

Snowbabies™

PLAYING GAMES IS FUN!

ITEM #	INTRO	STATUS	OSRP	GBTʀᴜ	↑
7947-2	1990	RETIRED 1993	$30.00	**$45.00**	7%

Product: Figurine
Material: Porcelain
Description: Snowbabies™ play London Bridge with penguins.
Particulars: Size is 5".

DATE:_____ $:_____		'91	'92	'93	'94	'95	'97
○ WISH	◑ HAVE	$30	32.5	32.5	55	45	42

A SPECIAL DELIVERY

ITEM #	INTRO	STATUS	OSRP	GBTʀᴜ	↓
7948-0	1990	RETIRED 1994	$13.50	**$24.00**	4%

Product: Figurine
Material: Porcelain
Description: Snowbaby on snowshoes delivers star.
Particulars: Size is 4".

DATE:_____ $:_____		'91	'92	'93	'94	'95	'97
○ WISH	○ HAVE	$13.5	14	15	15	18	25

WHO ARE YOU?

ITEM #	INTRO	STATUS	OSRP	GBTʀᴜ	↓
7949-9	1990	LTD ED 12,500	$32.50	**$100.00**	20%

Product: Figurine
Material: Porcelain
Description: Snowbaby and penguin with walrus.
Particulars: Size is 2.5". Early release to Gift Creations Concepts (GCC).

DATE:_____ $:_____		'91	'92	'93	'94	'95	'97
○ WISH	○ HAVE	$100	100	125	125	125	125

I'LL PUT UP THE TREE!

ITEM #	INTRO	STATUS	OSRP	GBTʀᴜ	↑
6800-4	1991	RETIRED 1995	$24.00	**$33.00**	10%

Product: Figurine
Material: Porcelain
Description: Snowbaby holds small tree with star.
Particulars: Size is 4". Early release to Gift Creations Concepts (GCC).

DATE:_____ $:_____		'91	'92	'93	'94	'95	'97
○ WISH	○ HAVE	$22	24	25	25	25	30

Snowbabies™

WHY DON'T YOU TALK TO ME?

Item #	Intro	Status	OSRP	GBTru	NO
6801-2	1991	Current	$22.00	**$24.00**	CHANGE

Product: Figurine
Material: Porcelain
Description: Snowbaby asks snowman a question.
Particulars: Size is 4".

DATE:_____ $:_____	'91	'92	'93	'94	'95	'97
○ WISH ● HAVE	$22	24	24	24	24	24

I MADE THIS JUST FOR YOU!

Item #	Intro	Status	OSRP	GBTru	NO
6802-0	1991	Current	$14.50	**$15.00**	CHANGE

Product: Figurine
Material: Porcelain
Description: Snowbaby carrying a star wreath.
Particulars: Size is 4.25".

DATE:_____ $:_____	'91	'92	'93	'94	'95	'97
○ WISH ○ HAVE	$14.5	15	15	15	15	15

IS THAT FOR ME?

Item #	Intro	Status	OSRP	GBTru	↑
6803-9	1991	Retired 1993	$30.00	**$48.00**	7%

Product: Figurines
Material: Porcelain
Description: One Snowbaby holds present for another.
Particulars: Set of 2. Size is 4.25".

DATE:_____ $:_____	'91	'92	'93	'94	'95	'97
○ WISH ○ HAVE	$30	32.5	32.5	50	50	45

POLAR SIGN

Item #	Intro	Status	OSRP	GBTru	↑
6804-7	1991	Retired 1996	$20.00	**$25.00**	4%

Product: Accessory
Material: Porcelain
Description: Penguin looks at collector's sign.
Particulars: Size is 3.5".

DATE:_____ $:_____	'91	'92	'93	'94	'95	'97
○ WISH ○ HAVE	$20	20	20	20	20	24

Snowbabies™

THIS IS WHERE WE LIVE!

ITEM #	INTRO	STATUS	OSRP	GBTRU	↓
6805-5	1991	RETIRED 1994	$55.00	**$70.00**	7%

Product: Figurine
Material: Porcelain
Description: Snowbaby shows walrus and polar bear The Pole.
Particulars: Size is 5".

DATE:_____ $:_____		'91	'92	'93	'94	'95	'97
○ WISH	◉ HAVE	$55	60	60	60	70	75

WAITING FOR CHRISTMAS

ITEM #	INTRO	STATUS	OSRP	GBTRU	↑
6807-1	1991	RETIRED 1993	$27.50	**$45.00**	13%

Product: Figurine
Material: Porcelain
Description: Two Snowbabies™ sitting on opposite sides of present–one watches, one naps.
Particulars: Size is 2.75".

DATE:_____ $:_____		'92	'93	'94	'95	'97
○ WISH	○ HAVE	$27.5	27.5	45	45	40

DANCING TO A TUNE

ITEM #	INTRO	STATUS	OSRP	GBTRU	↑
6808-0	1991	RETIRED 1995	$30.00	**$40.00**	5%

Product: Figurines
Material: Porcelain
Description: Snowbaby plays concertina as two Snowbabies™ dance.
Particulars: Set of 3. Size is 4".

DATE:_____ $:_____		'92	'93	'94	'95	'97
○ WISH	○ HAVE	$30	30	30	30	38

FISHING FOR DREAMS

ITEM #	INTRO	STATUS	OSRP	GBTRU	↑
6809-8	1991	RETIRED 1994	$28.00	**$44.00**	10%

Product: Figurine
Material: Porcelain
Description: Snowbaby ice fishing for a star watched by two puffins.
Particulars: Size is 4".

DATE:_____ $:_____		'92	'93	'94	'95	'97
○ WISH	○ HAVE	$28	28	28	38	40

Snowbabies™

SWINGING ON A STAR

ITEM #	INTRO	STATUS	OSRP	GBTRU	NO
6810-1	1991	CURRENT	$9.50	**$10.00**	CHANGE

Product: Ornament
Material: Porcelain
Description: Snowbaby seated on swing holds large star.
Particulars: Size is 3.5".

DATE:_____ $:_____		'92	'93	'94	'95	'97
○ WISH ◉ HAVE		$9.5	10	10	10	10

MY FIRST STAR

ITEM #	INTRO	STATUS	OSRP	GBTRU	NO
6811-0	1991	CURRENT	$7.00	**$7.50**	CHANGE

Product: Ornament
Material: Porcelain
Description: Snowbaby icicle with star ornament.
Particulars: Size is 6.75".

DATE:_____ $:_____		'92	'93	'94	'95	'97
○ WISH ◉ HAVE		$7	7.5	7.5	7.5	7.5

PLAYING GAMES IS FUN!

ITEM #	INTRO	STATUS	OSRP	GBTRU	↓
7632-5	1991	RETIRED 1993	$72.00	**$80.00**	24%

Product: Revolving Music Box
Material: Wood/Resin
Description: Snowbabies™ play London Bridge with two penguins.
Particulars: Tune: "Twinkle, Twinkle Little Star." Size is 6".

DATE:_____ $:_____		'92	'93	'94	'95	'97
○ WISH ○ HAVE		$72	72	NE	95	105

PENGUIN PARADE

ITEM #	INTRO	STATUS	OSRP	GBTRU	↑
7633-3	1991	RETIRED 1994	$72.00	**$80.00**	7%

Product: Revolving Music Box
Material: Wood/Resin
Description: One Snowbaby plays flute, one Snowbaby watches as penguins parade to tune.
Particulars: Tune: "Brahms' Lullaby." Size is 7".

DATE:_____ $:_____		'92	'93	'94	'95	'97
○ WISH ○ HAVE		$72	72	72	75	75

Snowbabies™

FROSTY FROLIC

ITEM #	INTRO	STATUS	OSRP	GBTʀᴜ	↓
7634-1	1991	RETIRED 1993	$110.00	**$165.00**	6%

Product: 2-Tier Music Box
Material: Wood/Resin
Description: Top Tier: Snowbabies™ circle tree. Bottom Tier: Snowbabies™ play instruments for penguins.
Particulars: Tune: "Let It Snow." Size is 10.25".

DATE:_____ $:_____			'92	'93	'94	'95	'97
○ WISH	○ HAVE		$110	110	NE	150	175

SNOWBABIES™ ADVENT TREE WITH 24 ORNAMENTS

ITEM #	INTRO	STATUS	OSRP	GBTʀᴜ	↓
7635-0	1991	RETIRED 1994	$135.00	**$165.00**	11%

Product: Music Box
Material: Wood/Sisal/Pewter
Description: Snowbabies™ advent tree with 24 ornaments.
Particulars: Set of 25. Tune: "We Wish You A Merry Christmas."

DATE:_____ $:_____			'92	'93	'94	'95	'97
○ WISH	○ HAVE		$135	135	135	150	185

PLAY ME A TUNE

ITEM #	INTRO	STATUS	OSRP	GBTʀᴜ	NO
7936-7	1991	RETIRED 1993	$50.00	**$65.00**	CHANGE

Product: Waterglobe, Music Box
Material: Bisque/Glass/Resin
Description: Snowbaby plays a horn as penguin listens.
Particulars: Tune: "We Wish You A Merry Christmas." Size is 5".

DATE:_____ $:_____			'92	'93	'94	'95	'97
○ WISH	○ HAVE		$50	50	75	65	65

PEEK-A-BOO

ITEM #	INTRO	STATUS	OSRP	GBTʀᴜ	↓
7938-3	1991	RETIRED 1993	$50.00	**$75.00**	6%

Product: Waterglobe, Music Box
Material: Bisque/Glass/Resin
Description: Snowbaby covers eyes with hands playing with penguins.
Particulars: Tune: "Jingle Bells." Size is 6.5".

DATE:_____ $:_____			'92	'93	'94	'95	'97
○ WISH	○ HAVE		$50	50	75	80	80

Snowbabies™

Can I Help, Too?

Item #	Intro	Status	OSRP	GBTru	↑
6806-3	1992	Ltd Ed 18,500	$48.00	**$80.00**	7%

Product: Figurine
Material: Porcelain
Description: Snowbaby seated on polar bear places star on tree. Second Snowbaby holds up another star. Penguin greets bear.
Particulars: Size is 5".

DATE:_____ $:_____	'92	'93	'94	'95	'97
◉ WISH ○ HAVE	$48	88	90	75	75

Wait For Me!

Item #	Intro	Status	OSRP	GBTru	↑
6812-8	1992	Retired 1994	$48.00	**$64.00**	7%

Product: Figurine
Material: Porcelain
Description: Snowbaby pushes sleigh filled with presents and stars as two penguins follow.
Particulars: Size is 4.5".

DATE:_____ $:_____	'92	'93	'94	'95	'97
◉ WISH ○ HAVE	$48	48	48	60	60

I Need A Hug

Item #	Intro	Status	OSRP	GBTru	NO
6813-6	1992	Current	$20.00	**$20.00**	CHANGE

Product: Figurine
Material: Porcelain
Description: Two Snowbabies™ hug.
Particulars: Size is 4.25".

DATE:_____ $:_____	'92	'93	'94	'95	'97
○ WISH ◉ HAVE	$20	20	20	20	20

Winken, Blinken, & Nod

Item #	Intro	Status	OSRP	GBTru	NO
6814-4	1992	Current	$60.00	**$65.00**	CHANGE

Product: Figurine
Material: Porcelain
Description: Three Snowbabies™ in star trimmed boat with waves lapping at base.
Particulars: Size is 5". Early release to Gift Creations Concepts (GCC).

DATE:_____ $:_____	'92	'93	'94	'95	'97
○ WISH ○ HAVE	$60	65	65	65	65

Snowbabies™

LET'S GO SKIING

ITEM #	INTRO	STATUS	OSRP	GBTRU	NO
6815-2	1992	CURRENT	$15.00	**$15.00**	CHANGE

Product: Figurine
Material: Porcelain
Description: Snowbaby holds skis.
Particulars: Size is 4.5".

DATE:_____ $:_____

		'92	'93	'94	'95	'97
○ WISH	● HAVE	$15	15	15	15	15

THIS WILL CHEER YOU UP

ITEM #	INTRO	STATUS	OSRP	GBTRU	↓
6816-0	1992	RETIRED 1994	$30.00	**$45.00**	4%

Product: Figurine
Material: Porcelain
Description: Snowbabies™ exchanging star.
Particulars: Size is 4.25". Early release to Ideation.

DATE:_____ $:_____

		'92	'93	'94	'95	'97
○ WISH	○ HAVE	$30	30	30	40	47

HELP ME, I'M STUCK!

ITEM #	INTRO	STATUS	OSRP	GBTRU	↑
6817-9	1992	RETIRED 1994	$32.50	**$50.00**	19%

Product: Figurine
Material: Porcelain
Description: Snowbaby under pile of stars gets helping hand.
Particulars: Size is 3.75".

DATE:_____ $:_____

		'93	'94	'95	'97
○ WISH	○ HAVE	$32.5	32.5	40	42

YOU CAN'T FIND ME!

ITEM #	INTRO	STATUS	OSRP	GBTRU	↑
6818-7	1992	RETIRED 1996	$45.00	**$52.00**	4%

Product: Figurine
Material: Porcelain
Description: Snowbabies™ with penguins playing hide-and-seek.
Particulars: Size is 5".

DATE:_____ $:_____

		'93	'94	'95	'97
● WISH	○ HAVE	$45	45	45	50

Snowbabies™

LOOK WHAT I CAN DO!

ITEM #	INTRO	STATUS	OSRP	GBTRU	↑
6819-5	1992	RETIRED 1996	$16.50	**$30.00**	25%

Product: Figurine
Material: Porcelain
Description: Snowbaby juggling stars.
Particulars: Size is 5".

DATE:_____ $:_____
○ WISH ● HAVE

	'93	'94	'95	'97
	$16.5	16.5	16.5	24

SHALL I PLAY FOR YOU?

ITEM #	INTRO	STATUS	OSRP	GBTRU	NO
6820-9	1992	CURRENT	$16.50	**$16.50**	CHANGE

Product: Figurine
Material: Porcelain
Description: Snowbaby playing drum.
Particulars: Size is 4".

DATE:_____ $:_____
○ WISH ○ HAVE

	'93	'94	'95	'97
	$16.5	16.5	16.5	16.5

YOU DIDN'T FORGET ME!

ITEM #	INTRO	STATUS	OSRP	GBTRU	NO
6821-7	1992	CURRENT	$32.50	**$32.50**	CHANGE

Product: Figurine
Material: Porcelain
Description: Snowbaby getting mail.
Particulars: Size is 4.5".

DATE:_____ $:_____
○ WISH ● HAVE

	'93	'94	'95	'97
	$32.5	32.5	32.5	32.5

STARS-IN-A-ROW, TIC-TAC-TOE

ITEM #	INTRO	STATUS	OSRP	GBTRU	↑
6822-5	1992	RETIRED 1995	$32.50	**$48.00**	26%

Product: Figurine
Material: Porcelain
Description: Snowbabies™ playing tic-tac-toe.
Particulars: Size is 4.5".

DATE:_____ $:_____
○ WISH ○ HAVE

	'93	'94	'95	'97
	$32.5	32.5	32.5	38

Snowbabies™

JUST ONE LITTLE CANDLE

ITEM #	INTRO	STATUS	OSRP	GBTru	
6823-3	1992	CURRENT	$15.00	**$15.00**	NO CHANGE

Product: Figurine
Material: Porcelain
Description: Snowbaby holding candle.
Particulars: Size is 4".

DATE:_____ $:_____

○ WISH   ◉ HAVE

	'93	'94	'95	'97
	$15	15	15	15

JOIN THE PARADE

ITEM #	INTRO	STATUS	OSRP	GBTru	
6824-1	1992	RETIRED 1994	$37.50	**$55.00**	↑ 10%

Product: Figurine
Material: Porcelain
Description: Snowbaby marching with friends.
Particulars: Size is 4.5".

DATE:_____ $:_____

○ WISH   ○ HAVE

	'93	'94	'95	'97
	$37.5	37.5	50	50

SNOWBABIES™ ICICLE WITH STAR

ITEM #	INTRO	STATUS	OSRP	GBTru	
6825-0	1992	RETIRED 1995	$16.00	**$20.00**	NO CHANGE

Product: Ornaments
Material: Porcelain
Description: Snowbabies™ icicle with star ornament.
Particulars: Set of 4. Size is 7.25".

DATE:_____ $:_____

○ WISH   ○ HAVE

	'93	'94	'95	'97
	$16	16	16	20

WHAT WILL I CATCH?

ITEM #	INTRO	STATUS	OSRP	GBTru	
6826-8	1992	CURRENT	$48.00	**$48.00**	NO CHANGE

Product: Music Box
Material: Porcelain
Description: Snowbaby fishing.
Particulars: Tune: "Catch A Falling Star." Size is 5.5".

DATE:_____ $:_____

◉ WISH   ○ HAVE

	'93	'94	'95	'97
	$48	48	48	48

Snowbabies™

OVER THE MILKY WAY

ITEM #	INTRO	STATUS	OSRP	GBTRU	↑
6828-4	1992	RETIRED 1995	$32.00	**$45.00**	13%

Product: Accessory
Material: Porcelain
Description: Snowbabies™ bridge.
Particulars: Size is 3".

DATE:_____ $:_____	'93	'94	'95	'97
○ WISH ○ HAVE	$32	32	32	40

STARRY PINES

ITEM #	INTRO	STATUS	OSRP	GBTRU	NO
6829-2	1992	CURRENT	$17.50	**$17.50**	CHANGE

Product: Accessories
Material: Porcelain
Description: Snowbabies™ trees.
Particulars: Set of 2. Sizes are 8.5" and 6.5".

DATE:_____ $:_____	'93	'94	'95	'97
○ WISH ○ HAVE	$17.5	17.5	17.5	17.5

STARRY, STARRY NIGHT

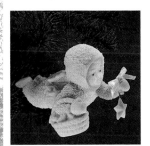

ITEM #	INTRO	STATUS	OSRP	GBTRU	NO
6830-6	1992	CURRENT	$12.50	**$12.50**	CHANGE

Product: Ornament
Material: Porcelain
Description: Snowbaby flying with basket of stars.
Particulars: Size is 4.5". Box reads: "Starry Night."

DATE:_____ $:_____	'93	'94	'95	'97
○ WISH ○ HAVE	$12.5	12.5	12.5	12.5

READ ME A STORY!

ITEM #	INTRO	STATUS	OSRP	GBTRU	↑
6831-4	1992	RETIRED 1996	$32.50	**$42.00**	20%

Product: Waterglobe, Music Box
Material: Bisque/Glass/Resin
Description: Snowbaby reading book to penguins.
Particulars: Tune: "Twinkle, Twinkle, Little Star." Size is 4".

DATE:_____ $:_____	'93	'94	'95	'97
○ WISH ○ HAVE	$32.5	32.5	32.5	35

Snowbabies™

FISHING FOR DREAMS

ITEM #	INTRO	STATUS	OSRP	GBTRU	↑
6832-2	1992	RETIRED 1994	$32.50	**$52.00**	4%

Product: Waterglobe, Music Box
Material: Bisque/Glass/Resin
Description: Snowbaby and puffins fishing.
Particulars: Tune: "Catch A Falling Star." Size is 4".

DATE:_____ $:_____

		'93	'94	'95	'97
○ WISH	○ HAVE	$32.5	32.5	45	50

LOOK WHAT I FOUND!

ITEM #	INTRO	STATUS	OSRP	GBTRU	↑
6833-0	1993	RETIRED 1997	$45.00	**$50.00**	11%

Product: Figurine
Material: Porcelain
Description: Two polar bear cubs in snow house shelter discovered by Snowbaby.
Particulars: Size is 3.75". Early release to Showcase Dealers and select buying groups.

DATE:_____ $:_____

		'93	'94	'95	'97
◉ WISH	○ HAVE	$45	45	45	45

CROSSING STARRY SKIES

ITEM #	INTRO	STATUS	OSRP	GBTRU	↑
6834-9	1993	RETIRED 1997	$35.00	**$40.00**	14%

Product: Figurine
Material: Porcelain
Description: Snowbaby paddles in kayak across star strewn ice.
Particulars: Size is 5". Early release to Showcase Dealers and select buying groups.

DATE:_____ $:_____

		'93	'94	'95	'97
○ WISH	○ HAVE	$35	35	35	35

I'LL TEACH YOU A TRICK

ITEM #	INTRO	STATUS	OSRP	GBTRU	↓
6835-7	1993	RETIRED 1996	$24.00	**$28.00**	7%

Product: Figurine
Material: Porcelain
Description: Snowbaby teaches penguin to jump through hoop.
Particulars: Size is 3.75". Early release to Showcase Dealers and select buying groups.

DATE:_____ $:_____

		'93	'94	'95	'97
○ WISH	○ HAVE	$24	24	24	30

Snowbabies™

I FOUND YOUR MITTENS!

ITEM #	INTRO	STATUS	OSRP	GBTRU	↑
6836-5	1993	RETIRED 1996	$30.00	**$35.00**	6%

Product: Figurines
Material: Porcelain
Description: Snowbaby holds mittens as second Snowbaby hugs cold hands to keep warm.
Particulars: Set of 2. Size is 4.25". Early release to Showcase Dealers and select buying groups.

DATE:_____ $:_____		'93	'94	'95	'97
○ WISH ● HAVE		$30	30	30	33

SO MUCH WORK TO DO!

ITEM #	INTRO	STATUS	OSRP	GBTRU	NO
6837-3	1993	CURRENT	$18.00	**$18.00**	CHANGE

Product: Figurine
Material: Porcelain
Description: Snowbaby gathers stars with a shovel.
Particulars: Size is 3.75". Early release to Showcase Dealers and select buying groups.

DATE:_____ $:_____		'93	'94	'95	'97
○ WISH ○ HAVE		$18	18	18	18

CAN I OPEN IT NOW?

ITEM #	INTRO	STATUS	OSRP	GBTRU	↓
6838-1	1993	EVENT PIECE	$15.00	**$30.00**	14%

Product: Figurine
Material: Porcelain
Description: Seated Snowbaby holds gift wrapped present.
Particulars: Size is 2.75". 1993 Event piece.

DATE:_____ $:_____		'93	'94	'95	'97
○ WISH ○ HAVE		$15	35	35	35

NOW I LAY ME DOWN TO SLEEP

ITEM #	INTRO	STATUS	OSRP	GBTRU	NO
6839-0	1993	CURRENT	$13.50	**$13.50**	CHANGE

Product: Figurine
Material: Porcelain
Description: Snowbaby says bedtime prayers.
Particulars: Size is 3.5".

DATE:_____ $:_____	'94	'95	'97
● WISH ○ HAVE	$13.5	13.5	13.5

Snowbabies™

SOMEWHERE IN DREAMLAND

ITEM #	INTRO	STATUS	OSRP	GBTRU	↑
6840-3	1993	RETIRED 1997	$85.00	**$95.00**	12%

Product: Figurine
Material: Porcelain
Description: Snowbabies™ nap on moon watched by bear, puffin and penguin.
Particulars: Size is 7.25". Year of production indicated by number of snowflakes on brass plate located on bottom. 1993–1; 1994–2; 1995–3; 1996–4; 1997–5.

DATE:_____ $:_____

			'94	'95	'97
● WISH	○ HAVE		$85	85	85

WHERE DID HE GO?

ITEM #	INTRO	STATUS	OSRP	GBTRU	NO
6841-1	1993	CURRENT	$35.00	**$35.00**	CHANGE

Product: Figurine
Material: Porcelain
Description: Snowbabies™ and penguin check melting snowman.
Particulars: Size is 4.25".

DATE:_____ $:_____

			'94	'95	'97
● WISH	○ HAVE		$35	35	35

I'M MAKING AN ICE SCULPTURE!

ITEM #	INTRO	STATUS	OSRP	GBTRU	↑
6842-0	1993	RETIRED 1996	$30.00	**$40.00**	14%

Product: Figurine
Material: Porcelain
Description: Snowbaby creates penguin ice sculpture.
Particulars: Size is 4.5". Originally shipped in boxes that read, "I'm An Artist."

DATE:_____ $:_____

			'94	'95	'97
○ WISH	○ HAVE		$30	30	35

WE MAKE A GREAT PAIR

ITEM #	INTRO	STATUS	OSRP	GBTRU	NO
6843-8	1993	CURRENT	$30.00	**$30.00**	CHANGE

Product: Figurine
Material: Porcelain
Description: Snowbaby friends ice skating.
Particulars: Size is 4".

DATE:_____ $:_____

			'94	'95	'97
○ WISH	○ HAVE		$30	30	30

Snowbabies™

WILL IT SNOW TODAY?

ITEM #	INTRO	STATUS	OSRP	GBTRU	NO
6844-6	1993	RETIRED 1995	$45.00	**$60.00**	CHANGE

Product: Figurine
Material: Porcelain
Description: Snowbaby, penguin and walrus check weather vane for forecast.
Particulars: Size is 6.25".

DATE:_____ $:_____		'94	'95	'97
○ WISH ○ HAVE		$45	45	60

LET'S ALL CHIME IN!

ITEM #	INTRO	STATUS	OSRP	GBTRU	↑
6845-4	1993	RETIRED 1995	$37.50	**$57.00**	14%

Product: Figurines
Material: Porcelain
Description: Three Snowbabies™ as bell ringers.
Particulars: Set of 2. Size is 4".

DATE:_____ $:_____		'94	'95	'97
○ WISH ○ HAVE		$37.5	37.5	50

BABY'S FIRST SMILE

ITEM #	INTRO	STATUS	OSRP	GBTRU	NO
6846-2	1993	CURRENT	$30.00	**$30.00**	CHANGE

Product: Picture Frame
Material: Porcelain
Description: Snowbaby and penguin admire picture in frame.
Particulars: Size is 6.5".

DATE:_____ $:_____		'94	'95	'97
◉ WISH ○ HAVE		$30	30	30

WEE ... THIS IS FUN!

ITEM #	INTRO	STATUS	OSRP	GBTRU	↑
6847-0	1993	RETIRED 1997	$13.50	**$20.00**	48%

Product: Ornament
Material: Porcelain
Description: Snowbaby slides down icicle.
Particulars: Size is 6.5".

DATE:_____ $:_____		'94	'95	'97
○ WISH ◉ HAVE		$13.5	13.5	13.5

Snowbabies™

SPRINKLING STARS IN THE SKY

ITEM #	INTRO	STATUS	OSRP	GBTRU	↑
6848-9	1993	RETIRED 1997	$12.50	**$20.00**	60%

Product: Ornament
Material: Porcelain
Description: Snowbaby releases stars into night sky.
Particulars: Size is 6.75".

DATE:_____ $:_____

○ WISH   ○ HAVE

'94	'95	'97
$12.5	12.5	12.5

SO MUCH WORK TO DO!

ITEM #	INTRO	STATUS	OSRP	GBTRU	↑
6849-7	1993	RETIRED 1995	$32.50	**$45.00**	18%

Product: Waterglobe, Music Box
Material: Bisque/Glass/Resin
Description: Snowbaby gathers stars with a shovel.
Particulars: Tune: "Whistle While You Work." Size is 6".

DATE:_____ $:_____

○ WISH   ○ HAVE

'94	'95	'97
$32.5	32.5	38

YOU DIDN'T FORGET ME!

ITEM #	INTRO	STATUS	OSRP	GBTRU	↑
6850-0	1993	RETIRED 1997	$32.50	**$45.00**	38%

Product: Waterglobe, Music Box
Material: Bisque/Glass/Resin
Description: Snowbaby getting mail.
Particulars: Tune: "Have Yourself A Merry Little Christmas." Size is 6".

DATE:_____ $:_____

○ WISH   ○ HAVE

'94	'95	'97
$32.5	32.5	32.5

I'M SO SLEEPY

ITEM #	INTRO	STATUS	OSRP	GBTRU	NO
6851-9	1993	CURRENT	$37.50	**$37.50**	CHANGE

Product: Revolving Music Box
Material: Porcelain
Description: Snowbaby naps on crescent moon.
Particulars: Tune: "Brahms' Lullaby." Size is 7".

DATE:_____ $:_____

○ WISH   ○ HAVE

'94	'95	'97
$37.5	37.5	37.5

Snowbabies™

SNOWBABIES™ ANIMATED BOOK MUSIC BOX

Item #	Intro	Status	OSRP	GBTru	↑
6857-8	1993	Retired 1995	$100.00	**$140.00**	12%

Product: Music Box
Material: Resin
Description: Snowbabies™ gathering and placing stars.
Particulars: Lighted. Tune: "Let It Snow." Battery operated.

DATE:_____ $:_____		'94	'95	'97
○ WISH ○ HAVE		$100	100	125

PENGUIN PARADE

Item #	Intro	Status	OSRP	GBTru	NO
7646-5	1993	Retired 1994	$20.00	**$40.00**	CHANGE

Product: Acrylic Music Box

Description: Snowbaby with flute & penguins.
Particulars: Tune: "Winter Wonderland." Size is 2.75".

DATE:_____ $:_____		'94	'95	'97
○ WISH ○ HAVE		$20	50	40

WISHING ON A STAR

Item #	Intro	Status	OSRP	GBTru	↓
7647-3	1993	Retired 1994	$20.00	**$40.00**	13%

Product: Acrylic Music Box

Description: Penguin watches Snowbaby holding up star
   to wish upon.
Particulars: Tune: "When You Wish Upon A Star."
   Size is 2.75".

DATE:_____ $:_____		'94	'95	'97
○ WISH ○ HAVE		$20	50	46

CAN I OPEN IT NOW?

Item #	Intro	Status	OSRP	GBTru	↓
7648-1	1993	Retired 1994	$20.00	**$40.00**	20%

Product: Acrylic Music Box

Description: Seated Snowbaby holds gift wrapped present.
Particulars: Tune: "Happy Birthday." Size is 2.75".

DATE:_____ $:_____		'94	'95	'97
○ WISH ○ HAVE		$20	50	50

Snowbabies™

Reading A Story

Item #	Intro	Status	OSRP	GBTru	↓
7649-0	1993	Retired 1994	$20.00	**$40.00**	9%

Product: Acrylic Music Box

Description: Snowbaby reading.
Particulars: Tune: "Brahms' Lullaby." Size is 2.75".

DATE:_____ $:_____	'94	'95	'97
○ WISH ○ HAVE	$20	50	44

Frosty Fun

Item #	Intro	Status	OSRP	GBTru	
7650-3	1993	Retired 1994	$20.00	**$40.00**	NO CHANGE

Product: Acrylic Music Box

Description: Snowbaby builds a snowman.
Particulars: Tune: "Frosty The Snowman." Size is 2.75".

DATE:_____ $:_____	'94	'95	'97
○ WISH ○ HAVE	$20	50	40

Play Me A Tune

Item #	Intro	Status	OSRP	GBTru	↓
7651-1	1993	Retired 1994	$20.00	**$40.00**	5%

Product: Acrylic Music Box

Description: Snowbaby plays a flute as penguin listens.
Particulars: Tune: "Joy To The World." Size is 2.75".

DATE:_____ $:_____	'94	'95	'97
○ WISH ○ HAVE	$20	50	42

Mickey's New Friend

Item #	Intro	Status	OSRP	GBTru	↓
714-5	1994	Retired 1995	$60.00	**$625.00**	10%

Product: Figurine
Material: Porcelain
Description: Disney's Fantasia Mickey touches a Snowbaby with his magic wand.
Particulars: Available for a limited time at Disney Parks. Originally, wand was glued to Mickey's hand. In later shipments, it was loose in the box.

DATE:_____ $:_____	'95	'97
○ WISH ○ HAVE	$500	695

Snowbabies™

I'M RIGHT BEHIND YOU!

ITEM #	INTRO	STATUS	OSRP	GBTRU	↑
6852-7	1994	RETIRED 1997	$60.00	**$65.00**	8%

Product: Figurine
Material: Porcelain
Description: Three Snowbabies™ on skates push Snowbaby on sled.
Particulars: Size is 2". Early release to National Association of Limited Edition Dealers (NALED).

DATE:_____ $:_____
○ WISH ○ HAVE

		'94	'95	'97
		$60	60	60

THERE'S ANOTHER ONE!

ITEM #	INTRO	STATUS	OSRP	GBTRU	NO
6853-5	1994	CURRENT	$24.00	**$24.00**	CHANGE

Product: Figurine
Material: Porcelain
Description: Snowbaby pushing wheelbarrow collecting stars.
Particulars: Size is 4.25". Early release to Ideation.

DATE:_____ $:_____
○ WISH ○ HAVE

		'94	'95	'97
		$24	24	24

JACK FROST ... A TOUCH OF WINTER'S MAGIC

ITEM #	INTRO	STATUS	OSRP	GBTRU	NO
6854-3	1994	CURRENT	$90.00	**$95.00**	CHANGE

Product: Figurine
Material: Porcelain
Description: Holding a star wand with stars, Jack Frost protects Snowbaby and friends from wind with his robe.
Particulars: Size is 10". Early release to Gift Creations Concepts (GCC).

DATE:_____ $:_____
○ WISH ○ HAVE

		'94	'95	'97
		$90	95	95

You Gotta Have Friends

Many of us have noticed that a number of Snowbabies™ have "friends" accompanying them on their designs. Have you ever wondered which friend was the most popular, and when all these different friends appeared?

The Snowbaby line started in 1986, but the very first non-Snowbaby to appear was the polar bear in *Polar Express* in 1988. This figurine, which retired in 1992, had two Snowbabies™ sitting atop a polar bear, going for a ride. At the time this was the most expensive Snowbaby in the current line at $22, excluding the waterglobe *Snowbabies™ Riding Sleds* which retired that same year. *Polar Express* sells for about $85 on the secondary market. *(continued page 56)*

Snowbabies™

The following year, we got our first glimpse of two new friends, the penguin and the snowman. Two designs with penguins attached were made available in 1989. One was named *Helpful Friends* and sold for $30 while the other was called *Penguin Parade* and had a price tag of $25. Both sets of penguins were busy playing and helping the Snowbabies™. The other new friend was not a biological creature at all, but a snowman. *Frosty Fun* would prove to be the first of the six snowman-related figures to be available in the line. In this piece two Snowbabies™ are putting the finishing touches on a snowman that they just built.

In 1990 the third limited edition for the Snowbabies™ line was produced. This scene was called *Who Are You?* and premiered a new animal, the walrus. This figurine was an early release to retailers belonging to the Gift Creations Concepts catalogue buying group (GCC) and was limited to 12,500 pieces. It sold for $32.50, and on the secondary market today it's valued at $100.

Just when we thought Department 56, Inc. couldn't think up more friends for the North Pole, it introduced *Fishing For Dreams*, the first Snowbabies™ piece to have a puffin on it. Puffins may not have been familiar to most of us, but since its arrival in 1991 there have been 10 more figurines that have included them.

We waited a few years before another non-Snowbaby would make his appearance. Boy, was it worth the wait! *Jack Frost…A Touch Of Winter's Magic* was a 1994 release commanding a high price tag. This was the most expensive Snowbabies™ piece that had been produced up to that time and exhibited the first person ever to be seen in the Snowbabies™ line. This, too, was an early release to GCC and stands about 10" tall.

In that same year, but arriving with much less fanfare, was the *Where Did You Come From?* Snowbabies™ sign. It showed a Snowbaby constructing an ice block sign when a bunny comes up beside him. The bunny must certainly have been lost because it is only one of two bunnies in the collection to date. Many people speculated that the older Snowbabies™ sign would retire in 1994 since this new sign had been introduced. But, the old sign called *Polar Sign* stayed in the line until 1996. The new sign sells for twice the retail of the original one with the first being sold at $20.

Even Mickey Mouse became a friend of the Snowbabies™ in 1994 when *Mickey's New Friend* was introduced. Available only at the Disney theme parks, this popular design was only in the line for a short time. It retired in 1995.

1995 saw the most recent addition to the list of friends with *Mush!* This 12" long scene shows two Snowbabies™ on a snow sled being pulled by two huskies. Although this new animal has only been in the line since 1995, there are three designs which show these fun dogs.

the **Village Chronicle**.

Now that we have chronicled the arrivals of the different friends, we need to answer the question of which is the most popular. Well, if you're a Snowbabies™ collector, you know that answer without counting. It's the penguin, of course. This animal has appeared in 48 Snowbabies™ figurines (not including lite-ups, miniatures, or advent tree). The next closest contender is the polar bear with 17 and then the puffin with 11. What happened to Mr. Snowman? He came in fourth, it's sad to say.

The song says "You gotta have friends…" and the Snowbabies™ do. But if calculations are right, Department 56, Inc. should be adding a new friend or two in the near future. What will it be? Will it be another person, or perhaps a seal, a wolf, an owl…or…or…?

Snowbabies™

GATHERING STARS IN THE SKY

ITEM #	INTRO	STATUS	OSRP	GBTRU	↑
6855-1	1994	RETIRED 1997	$12.50	**$20.00**	60%

Product: Ornament
Material: Porcelain
Description: Snowbaby floating on a star to collect more stars.
Particulars: Size is 3".

DATE:_____ $:_____
○ WISH ○ HAVE

	'94	'95	'97
	$12.5	12.5	12.5

WHERE DID YOU COME FROM?

ITEM #	INTRO	STATUS	OSRP	GBTRU	↑
6856-0	1994	RETIRED 1997	$40.00	**$50.00**	25%

Product: Figurine
Material: Porcelain
Description: Snowbaby asks rabbit question while building ice block sign wall.
Particulars: Size is 5". Early release to Retail Resources.

DATE:_____ $:_____
○ WISH ○ HAVE

	'94	'95	'97
	$40	40	40

FIRST STAR JINGLEBABY

ITEM #	INTRO	STATUS	OSRP	GBTRU	↑
6858-6	1994	RETIRED 1997	$10.00	**$16.00**	45%

Product: Ornament
Material: Porcelain
Description: Snowbaby as a jingle bell carries first star of night.
Particulars: Size is 3.5".

DATE:_____ $:_____
○ WISH ○ HAVE

	'94	'95	'97
	$10	11	11

LITTLE DRUMMER JINGLEBABY

ITEM #	INTRO	STATUS	OSRP	GBTRU	↑
6859-4	1994	RETIRED 1997	$10.00	**$16.00**	45%

Product: Ornament
Material: Porcelain
Description: Snowbaby as a jingle bell plays a drum.
Particulars: Size is 3.5".

DATE:_____ $:_____
○ WISH ○ HAVE

	'94	'95	'97
	$10	11	11

Snowbabies™

LET'S GO SKATING

ITEM #	INTRO	STATUS	OSRP	GBTRU	NO
6860-8	1994	CURRENT	$16.50	**$16.50**	CHANGE

Product: Figurine
Material: Porcelain
Description: Snowbaby holding ice skates in hands.
Particulars: Size is 3.75".

DATE:_____ $:_____
O WISH ●HAVE

	'95	'97
	$16.5	16.5

STRINGING FALLEN STARS

ITEM #	INTRO	STATUS	OSRP	GBTRU	NO
6861-6	1994	CURRENT	$25.00	**$25.00**	CHANGE

Product: Figurine
Material: Porcelain
Description: Snowbaby strings stars from a box.
Particulars: Size is 4".

DATE:_____ $:_____
O WISH O HAVE

	'95	'97
	$25	25

BRINGING STARRY PINES

ITEM #	INTRO	STATUS	OSRP	GBTRU	↑
6862-4	1994	RETIRED 1997	$35.00	**$45.00**	29%

Product: Figurine
Material: Porcelain
Description: Snowbaby pulls a sled loaded with three
small pines.
Particulars: Size is 4".

DATE:_____ $:_____
O WISH O HAVE

	'95	'97
	$35	35

LIFT ME HIGHER, I CAN'T REACH!

ITEM #	INTRO	STATUS	OSRP	GBTRU	NO
6863-2	1994	CURRENT	$75.00	**$75.00**	CHANGE

Product: Figurine
Material: Porcelain
Description: One Snowbaby lifts another to place a star
on the tree.
Particulars: Size is 9".

DATE:_____ $:_____
O WISH O HAVE

	'95	'97
	$75	75

Snowbabies™

PENNIES FROM HEAVEN

ITEM #	INTRO	STATUS	OSRP	GBTRU	NO
6864-0	1994	CURRENT	$17.50	**$17.50**	CHANGE

Product: Bank
Material: Porcelain
Description: Storybook Bank.
Particulars: Size is 5".

DATE:_____ $:_____

		'95	'97
○ WISH	○ HAVE	$17.5	17.5

WE'LL PLANT THE STARRY PINES

ITEM #	INTRO	STATUS	OSRP	GBTRU	↑
6865-9	1994	RETIRED 1997	$37.50	**$40.00**	7%

Product: Figurines
Material: Porcelain
Description: Snowbabies™ plant tree as another holds next tree.
Particulars: Set of 2. Size is 4.25".

DATE:_____ $:_____

		'95	'97
○ WISH	○ HAVE	$37.5	37.5

BE MY BABY

ITEM #	INTRO	STATUS	OSRP	GBTRU	NO
6866-7	1994	CURRENT	$15.00	**$15.00**	CHANGE

Product: Block Ornament
Material: Porcelain
Description: An ornament celebrating Baby's First Christmas.
Particulars: Size is 2.25".

DATE:_____ $:_____

		'95	'97
○ WISH	○ HAVE	$15	15

JUGGLING STARS IN THE SKY

ITEM #	INTRO	STATUS	OSRP	GBTRU	NO
6867-5	1994	CURRENT	$15.00	**$15.00**	CHANGE

Product: Ornament
Material: Porcelain
Description: Sitting Snowbaby Juggles stars.
Particulars: Size is 5.25".

DATE:_____ $:_____

		'95	'97
○ WISH	○ HAVE	$15	15

Snowbabies™

STARS IN MY STOCKING JINGLEBABY

ITEM #	INTRO	STATUS	OSRP	GBTru	
6868-3	1994	CURRENT	$11.00	**$11.00**	NO CHANGE

Product: Ornament
Material: Porcelain
Description: Snowbaby counts the stars in Christmas stocking.
Particulars: Size is 3.75".

DATE:_____ $:_____	'95	'97
○ WISH ○ HAVE	$11	11

JUST FOR YOU JINGLEBABY

ITEM #	INTRO	STATUS	OSRP	GBTru	
6869-1	1994	CURRENT	$11.00	**$11.00**	NO CHANGE

Product: Ornament
Material: Porcelain
Description: Snowbaby presents a wreath of stars.
Particulars: Size is 3.25".

DATE:_____ $:_____	'95	'97
○ WISH ○ HAVE	$11	11

PLANTING STARRY PINES

ITEM #	INTRO	STATUS	OSRP	GBTru	
6870-5	1994	RETIRED 1996	$32.50	**$45.00**	↑ 13%

Product: Waterglobe, Music Box
Material: Bisque/Glass/Resin
Description: Snowbaby plants a pine tree.
Particulars: Tune: "O Tannenbaum." Size is 6".

DATE:_____ $:_____	'95	'97
○ WISH ○ HAVE	$32.5	40

CATCH A FALLING STAR

ITEM #	INTRO	STATUS	OSRP	GBTru	
6871-3	1994	RETIRED 1997	$37.50	**$42.00**	↑ 12%

Product: Music Box
Material: Porcelain
Description: Snowbaby catches a fallen star as a penguin and puffin look on.
Particulars: Tune: "Catch A Falling Star." Size is 8.75".

DATE:_____ $:_____	'95	'97
○ WISH ○ HAVE	$37.5	37.5

Snowbabies™

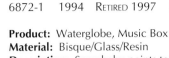

LOOK WHAT I FOUND!

ITEM #	INTRO	STATUS	OSRP	GBTru	↑
6872-1	1994	RETIRED 1997	$32.50	**$40.00**	23%

Product: Waterglobe, Music Box
Material: Bisque/Glass/Resin
Description: Snowbaby points to a bear cub.
Particulars: Tune: "Winter Wonderland." Size is 6".

DATE:_____ $:_____		'95	'97
○ WISH ○ HAVE		$32.5	32.5

"WINTER TALES OF THE SNOWBABIES"

ITEM #	INTRO	STATUS	OSRP	GBTru	NO
6873-0	1994	CURRENT	$18.95	**$18.95**	CHANGE

Product: Book

Description: Poems and drawings of Snowbabies™ and friends. 72-page hard-bound storybook. Size is 8.5" x 10".

DATE:_____ $:_____		'95	'97
○ WISH ○ HAVE		$18.95	18.95

OVERNIGHT DELIVERY

ITEM #	INTRO	STATUS	OSRP	GBTru	↓
759-5	1995	EVENT PIECE	$10.00	**$28.00**	38%

Product: Ornament
Material: Porcelain
Description: Flying Snowbaby delivers gift.
Particulars: Size is 5.5". Special Event piece for Retail Resources, for October 1995 Collector's Month. Ribbon on Ornament was gold. (Available to other retailers in 1996 with unpainted ribbon. See Item #68808, page 66.)

DATE:_____ $:_____	'97
○ WISH ○ HAVE	$45

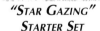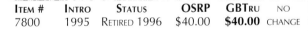

"STAR GAZING" STARTER SET

ITEM #	INTRO	STATUS	OSRP	GBTru	NO
7800	1995	RETIRED 1996	$40.00	**$40.00**	CHANGE

Product: Figurines/Accessories
Material: Porcelain
Description: Contains: I See You! (Set/2), Parade Of Penguins (Set/3), Frosty Pines (Set/3), 1.5 oz. Bag Of Real Plastic Snow.
Particulars: Set of 9. Starter Set exclusive to GCC & May Co. Figurines & accessories are existing product, packaging is new. (Available to other retailers in '96. See Item #68817, pg. 68.)

DATE:_____ $:_____	'97
○ WISH ○ HAVE	$40

Snowbabies™

I Found The Biggest Star Of All!

Item #	Intro	Status	OSRP	GBTru	
6874-8	1995	Current	$16.00	**$16.00**	NO CHANGE

Product: Figurine
Material: Porcelain
Description: Snowbaby holds up a giant star.
Particulars: Size is 4".

DATE:_____ $:_____

○ WISH   ○ HAVE

'95	'97
$16	16

Are You On My List?

Item #	Intro	Status	OSRP	GBTru	
6875-6	1995	Current	$25.00	**$25.00**	NO CHANGE

Product: Figurine
Material: Porcelain
Description: Snowbaby checks list for puffin's name.
Particulars: Size is 4.5". Midyear '95 early release to Ideation. Available to other retailers in 1996.

DATE:_____ $:_____

○ WISH   ◉ HAVE

'95	'97
$25	25

Ring The Bells ... It's Christmas!

Item #	Intro	Status	OSRP	GBTru	
6876-4	1995	Current	$40.00	**$40.00**	NO CHANGE

Product: Figurine
Material: Porcelain
Description: Snowbabies™ ring bell.
Particulars: Size is 5.25" x 6.5". Midyear '95 early release to Gift Creations Concepts (GCC). Available to other retailers in 1996.

DATE:_____ $:_____

○ WISH   ○ HAVE

'95	'97
$40	40

What Shall We Do Today?

Item #	Intro	Status	OSRP	GBTru	
6877-2	1995	Retired 1997	$32.50	**$42.00**	↑ 29%

Product: Figurine
Material: Porcelain
Description: Snowbaby leans on ice wall and asks penguins what plans can they make for the day.
Particulars: Midyear '95 early release to National Association of Limited Edition Dealers (NALED). Available to other retailers 1996.

DATE:_____ $:_____

○ WISH   ○ HAVE

'95	'97
$32.5	32.5

Snowbabies™

I See You!

Item #	Intro	Status	OSRP	GBTru	
6878-0	1995	Current	$27.50	**$27.50**	NO CHANGE

Product: Figurines
Material: Porcelain
Description: Snowbaby looks through telescope.
Particulars: Set of 2. Size is 4.5". Midyear '95 early release to Retail Resources. Available to other retailers in 1996.

			'95	'97
DATE:_____ $:_____			$27.5	27.5
○ WISH ○ HAVE				

Are You On My List?

Item #	Intro	Status	OSRP	GBTru	↑
6879-7	1995	Retired 1997	$32.50	**$42.00**	29%

Product: Waterglobe, Music Box
Material: Bisque/Glass/Resin
Description: Snowbaby checks list for the Puffin's name.
Particulars: Tune: "Have Yourself A Merry Little Christmas." Size is 6".

	'97
DATE:_____ $:_____	$32.5
○ WISH ○ HAVE	

I'll Hug You Goodnight

Item #	Intro	Status	OSRP	GBTru	
68798	1995	Current	$32.50	**$32.50**	NO CHANGE

Product: Waterglobe, Music Box
Material: Bisque/Glass/Resin
Description: Snowbaby hugs a snowman.
Particulars: Tune: "Frosty The Snowman." Size is 6".

	'97
DATE:_____ $:_____	$32.5
○ WISH ○ HAVE	

Skate With Me

Item #	Intro	Status	OSRP	GBTru	
68799	1995	Current	$32.50	**$32.50**	NO CHANGE

Product: Waterglobe, Music Box
Material: Bisque/Glass/Resin
Description: Snowbaby asks penguin to skate across the ice together.
Particulars: Tune: "Skater's Waltz." Size is 6".

	'97
DATE:_____ $:_____	$32.5
○ WISH ○ HAVE	

Snowbabies™

I Can't Find Him!

Item #	Intro	Status	OSRP	GBTru	
68800	1995	Current	$37.50	**$37.50**	NO CHANGE

Product: Figurine
Material: Porcelain
Description: One Snowbaby peeks into ice hole to spy on walrus. Second baby finds walrus behind them watching their activity.
Particulars: Size is 7.25".

DATE:_____ $:_____
○ WISH   ○ HAVE

'97
$37.5

I'll Play A Christmas Tune

Item #	Intro	Status	OSRP	GBTru	
68801	1995	Current	$16.00	**$16.00**	NO CHANGE

Product: Figurine
Material: Porcelain
Description: Sitting on a drum, a Snowbaby plays a piccolo.
Particulars: Size is 4.75".

DATE:_____ $:_____
○ WISH   ○ HAVE

'97
$16

We're Building An Icy Igloo

Item #	Intro	Status	OSRP	GBTru	
68802	1995	Current	$70.00	**$70.00**	NO CHANGE

Product: Figurine
Material: Porcelain
Description: Polar bear watches as two Snowbabies™ add final blocks to icy igloo.
Particulars: Lighted.

DATE:_____ $:_____
○ WISH   ○ HAVE

'97
$70

A Star-In-The-Box

Item #	Intro	Status	OSRP	GBTru	
68803	1995	Event Piece	$18.00	**$28.00**	↑ 56%

Product: Figurine
Material: Porcelain
Description: Snowbaby holding up stars pops out of a box like a jack-in-the box.
Particulars: Gift Creations Concepts (GCC) Exclusive National Open House Event piece, May 1996. Also available in Canada.

DATE:_____ $:_____
○ WISH   ○ HAVE

'97
$18

Snowbabies™

PARADE OF PENGUINS

ITEM #	INTRO	STATUS	OSRP	GBTRU	NO
68804	1995	CURRENT	$15.00	**$15.00**	CHANGE

Product: Figurines
Material: Porcelain
Description: Penguins looking up and around, doing penguin poses.
Particulars: Set of 6. Size is 2.5".

DATE:_____ $:_____

○ WISH ○ HAVE

'97
$15

MUSH!

ITEM #	INTRO	STATUS	OSRP	GBTRU	NO
68805	1995	CURRENT	$48.00	**$48.00**	CHANGE

Product: Figurines
Material: Porcelain
Description: Snowbabies™ on snow sled give 'go' command to two husky pups.
Particulars: Set of 2. Size is 4.25" to 12".

DATE:_____ $:_____

○ WISH ○ HAVE

'97
$48

ONE LITTLE CANDLE JINGLEBABY

ITEM #	INTRO	STATUS	OSRP	GBTRU	NO
68806	1995	CURRENT	$11.00	**$11.00**	CHANGE

Product: Ornament
Material: Porcelain
Description: Jingle bell Snowbaby holds lit candle.
Particulars: Size is 3.75".

DATE:_____ $:_____

○ WISH ○ HAVE

'97
$11

JOY

ITEM #	INTRO	STATUS	OSRP	GBTRU	NO
68807	1995	CURRENT	$32.50	**$32.50**	CHANGE

Product: Ornaments
Material: Porcelain
Description: Snowbaby on letter J plays horn; Snowbaby on Letter O holds star; Snowbaby on letter Y rings a bell.
Particulars: Set of 3. Size is 3.75".

DATE:_____ $:_____

○ WISH ○ HAVE

'97
$32.5

Snowbabies™

OVERNIGHT DELIVERY

ITEM #	INTRO	STATUS	OSRP	GBTru	NO
68808	1995	CURRENT	$10.00	**$10.00**	CHANGE

Product: Ornament
Material: Porcelain
Description: Flying Snowbaby delivers gift.
Particulars: Size is 5.5". Unpainted ribbon version available to all retailers. (See Item #759-5, page 61, for Retail Resources October 1995 Collector's Month Event piece with gold ribbon.)

DATE:_____ $:_____
○ WISH   ● HAVE

'97
$10

PLAY ME A TUNE

ITEM #	INTRO	STATUS	OSRP	GBTru	NO
68809	1995	CURRENT	$37.50	**$37.50**	CHANGE

Product: Music Box
Material: Porcelain
Description: Snowbabies™ seated on a drum play music. One taps a drum while the other blows a horn.
Particulars: Tune: "Little Drummer Boy." Size is 5.75".

DATE:_____ $:_____
○ WISH   ○ HAVE

'97
$37.5

ANIMATED SKATING POND

ITEM #	INTRO	STATUS	OSRP	GBTru	NO
7668-6	1995	CURRENT	$60.00	**$60.00**	CHANGE

Product: Accessory
Material: Resin & Sisal
Description: Snowbabies™ and friends skate around a pond as another Snowbaby kayaks in the open waters.
Particulars: Set of 14. Size is 17.5" x 14". Electric.

DATE:_____ $:_____
○ WISH   ○ HAVE

'95   '97
$60   60

FROSTY PINES

ITEM #	INTRO	STATUS	OSRP	GBTru	NO
76687	1995	CURRENT	$12.50	**$12.50**	CHANGE

Product: Accessories
Material: Sisal
Description: Three graduated size white sisal brush trees for display use.
Particulars: Set of 3. Sizes range from 4.5" to 7.5".

DATE:_____ $:_____
○ WISH   ○ HAVE

'97
$12.5

Snowbabies™

I'M SO SLEEPY

ITEM #	INTRO	STATUS	OSRP	GBTRu	NO
68810	1996	CURRENT	$16.00	**$16.00**	CHANGE

Product: Figurine
Material: Porcelain
Description: A sleepy Snowbaby yawns while holding a candle and special blanket.
Particulars: Size is 4.25". Midyear release.

DATE:_____ $:_____   '97
○ WISH   ○ HAVE $16

JACK FROST ... A SLEIGHRIDE THROUGH THE STARS

ITEM #	INTRO	STATUS	OSRP	GBTRu	NO
68811	1996	CURRENT	$110.00	**$110.00**	CHANGE

Product: Figurines
Material: Porcelain
Description: Snowbaby riding first of two polar bears leads the way for bear to pull sleigh with Jack Frost and two Snowbabies™.
Particulars: Set of 3. Size range is 7.5" to 20.75". Midyear release.

DATE:_____ $:_____   '97
○ WISH   ○ HAVE $110

WHICH WAY'S UP?

ITEM #	INTRO	STATUS	OSRP	GBTRu	↑
68812	1996	RETIRED 1997	$30.00	**$40.00**	33%

Product: Figurine
Material: Porcelain
Description: Snowbaby standing on head with the help of a friend as penguin watches.
Particulars: Size is 4.25". Midyear release.

DATE:_____ $:_____   '97
○ WISH   ○ HAVE $30

WITH HUGS & KISSES

ITEM #	INTRO	STATUS	OSRP	GBTRu	NO
68813	1996	CURRENT	$32.50	**$32.50**	CHANGE

Product: Figurines
Material: Porcelain
Description: Snowbaby takes star from his mailbag and delivers it to friend.
Particulars: Set of 2. Size is 4". Midyear release.

DATE:_____ $:_____   '97
○ WISH   ○ HAVE $32.5

Snowbabies™

YOU ARE MY LUCKY STAR

ITEM #	INTRO	STATUS	OSRP	GBTRU	NO
68814	1996	CURRENT	$35.00	**$35.00**	CHANGE

Product: Figurines
Material: Porcelain
Description: Snowbaby and polar bear cub listen as a Snowbaby plays a song on the violin.
Particulars: Set of 2. Midyear release.

DATE:_____ $:_____   '97
O WISH   O HAVE $35

ONCE UPON A TIME …

ITEM #	INTRO	STATUS	OSRP	GBTRU	NO
68815	1996	CURRENT	$25.00	**$25.00**	CHANGE

Product: Figurines/Votive Cup
Material: Porcelain/Glass
Description: Snowbaby reads a story to penguin pals showing them the pictures in the storybook.
Particulars: Midyear release.

DATE:_____ $:_____   '97
O WISH   O HAVE $25

CLIMB EVERY MOUNTAIN

ITEM #	INTRO	STATUS	OSRP	GBTRU	↓
68816	1996	LTD ED 22,500	$75.00	**$115.00**	21%

Product: Figurine
Material: Porcelain
Description: Snowbabies™ connected by golden chains pull a small sled.
Particulars: Size is 11" x 4.5" x 6". Midyear release. Limited Edition released in Canada through Millard Lister Sales Ltd. Approximately 150 pieces reserved for Canada.

DATE:_____ $:_____   '97
O WISH   O HAVE $145

STARGAZING

ITEM #	INTRO	STATUS	OSRP	GBTRU	NO
68817	1996	CURRENT	$40.00	**$40.00**	CHANGE

Product: Figurines/Accessories
Material: Porcelain
Description: Contains the following: I See You! (Set/2), Parade Of Penguins (Set/3), Frosty Pines (Set/3), 1.5 oz Bag Of Real Plastic Snow.
Particulars: Set of 9. (See Item #7800, page 61, "Star Gazing Starter Set" was exclusive to GCC and May Co.)

DATE:_____ $:_____   '97
O WISH   O HAVE $40

You Need Wings Too!

Item #	Intro	Status	OSRP	GBTru	NO
68818	1996	Current	$25.00	**$25.00**	CHANGE

Product: Figurine
Material: Porcelain
Description: Snowbaby places wings on snowman.
Particulars: Size is 4".

DATE:_____ $:_____
○ WISH ○ HAVE

'97
$25

When The Bough Breaks

Item #	Intro	Status	OSRP	GBTru	NO
68819	1996	Current	$30.00	**$30.00**	CHANGE

Product: Figurine
Material: Porcelain
Description: Snowbaby on a swing suspended between two pine trees.
Particulars: Size is 6"

DATE:_____ $:_____
○ WISH ● HAVE

'97
$30

There's No Place Like Home

Item #	Intro	Status	OSRP	GBTru	NO
68820	1996	Current	$16.50	**$16.50**	CHANGE

Product: Figurine
Material: Porcelain
Description: Snowbaby carries star package on a pole.
Particulars: Size is 4".

DATE:_____ $:_____
○ WISH ○ HAVE

'97
$16.5

It's Snowing!

Item #	Intro	Status	OSRP	GBTru	NO
68821	1996	Current	$16.50	**$16.50**	CHANGE

Product: Figurine
Material: Porcelain
Description: Snowbaby balances snowflake on foot.
Particulars: Size is 4".

DATE:_____ $:_____
○ WISH ○ HAVE

'97
$16.5

Snowbabies™

IT'S A GRAND OLD FLAG

ITEM #	INTRO	STATUS	OSRP	GBTRU	NO
68822	1996	CURRENT	$25.00	**$25.00**	CHANGE

Product: Figurine
Material: Porcelain
Description: Penguin watches Snowbaby carry flag.
Particulars: Size is 4" figurine, 8" flag. Though intended to be distributed in Canada, France, Germany, Great Britain, Italy, Japan, the Netherlands, and the U.S., it was only sold in Canada, Germany, Great Britain, and the United States. The Canada, Germany and Great Britain versions were retired in 1997. Each version displayed the flag of the appropriate country as well as the Snowbabies™ flag. The U.S. version is still current. The first U.S. release contained the U.S. and Snowbabies™ flags. The second version has only the Snowbabies™ flag.

DATE:_____ $:_____

O WISH   O HAVE

'97
$25

A LITTLE NIGHT LIGHT

ITEM #	INTRO	STATUS	OSRP	GBTRU	NO
68823	1996	CURRENT	$32.50	**$32.50**	CHANGE

Product: Figurine
Material: Porcelain
Description: Three Snowbabies™ carrying candles.
Particulars: Size is 4.5".

DATE:_____ $:_____

O WISH   O HAVE

'97
$32.5

FIVE-PART HARMONY

ITEM #	INTRO	STATUS	OSRP	GBTRU	NO
68824	1996	CURRENT	$45.00	**$45.00**	CHANGE

Product: Figurine
Material: Porcelain
Description: Four Snowbabies™ and a Husky puppy sing harmony.
Particulars: Size is 5".

DATE:_____ $:_____

O WISH   O HAVE

'97
$45

Snowbabies™

Keep Your Eyes on Those
Grand Old Flags

In December of 1996, Department 56, Inc. introduced *It's a Grand Old Flag,* featuring a Snowbaby carrying a flag. The news which accompanied the introduction quickly captured collectors' attention. This piece, it was announced, would be the first that Department 56, Inc. would distribute in Europe and Asia. The company's intentions were to make the piece available to a total of eight countries—Canada, Germany, Great Britain, Italy, France, Japan, the Netherlands, and the United States.

A creative aspect to the marketing plan for this particular design was that each Snowbaby would carry the flag of the appropriate country. In the U.S., the Snowbaby would include both the U.S. flag and the Snowbabies™ flag for the first year only, however. In subsequent years, it would include the "Snowbabies™" flag only.

The same was planned for the other countries, but it didn't turn out this way…at least not for all seven of the foreign countries. In fact, no shipment ever took place for four of the intended nations. The only countries other than the U.S. to receive the Snowbaby were Canada, Germany, and Great Britain. Then in December 1997, the versions produced for those three countries were retired, leaving only the U.S. version.

If you hope to find the foreign versions, you may still have some luck if you have a means of locating the Snowbaby and purchasing it in those countries. You never know, there could still be some on the shelves in stores that sold them. Perhaps you know someone who could pick one up for you, or maybe you'll be visiting one of the countries soon and will be able to look for yourself.

In any case, the international versions of *It's a Grand Old Flag* could turn out to be some of the rarest pieces of Snowbabies™ produced in recent years. Of course only time will tell, but since they were only available in those countries where there are few established Snowbabies™ collectors and only available for one year, it doesn't seem likely that there will be an abundance of them making their way back to the U.S.

the **Village Chronicle.**

Snowbabies™

STARRY PINE JINGLEBABY

ITEM #	INTRO	STATUS	OSRP	GBTru	NO
68825	1996	CURRENT	$11.00	**$11.00**	CHANGE

Product: Ornament
Material: Porcelain
Description: Snowbaby jinglebaby holds tiny pine tree.
Particulars: Size is 4".

DATE:_____ $:_____
○ WISH   ○ HAVE

'97
$11

JINGLEBELL JINGLEBABY

ITEM #	INTRO	STATUS	OSRP	GBTru	NO
68826	1996	CURRENT	$11.00	**$11.00**	CHANGE

Product: Ornament
Material: Porcelain
Description: Snowbaby jinglebaby holds jingle bells on a ribbon.
Particulars: Size is 3.5".

DATE:_____ $:_____
○ WISH   ○ HAVE

'97
$11

SNOWBABY IN MY STOCKING

ITEM #	INTRO	STATUS	OSRP	GBTru	NO
68827	1996	CURRENT	$10.00	**$10.00**	CHANGE

Product: Ornament
Material: Porcelain
Description: Snowbaby tucked into Christmas stocking.
Particulars: Size is 4".

DATE:_____ $:_____
○ WISH   ○ HAVE

'97
$10

BABY'S 1ST RATTLE

ITEM #	INTRO	STATUS	OSRP	GBTru	NO
68828	1996	CURRENT	$15.00	**$15.00**	CHANGE

Product: Ornament
Material: Porcelain
Description: Snowbaby tops baby rattle handle.
Particulars: Size is 5.5".

DATE:_____ $:_____
○ WISH   ○ HAVE

'97
$15

Snowbabies™

JOY TO THE WORLD

ITEM #	INTRO	STATUS	OSRP	GBTRU	NO
68829	1996	CURRENT	$16.50	**$16.50**	CHANGE

Product: Ornament
Material: Porcelain
Description: Snowbaby atop the world holds staff and pennant.
Particulars: Set of 2. Size is 6".

DATE:_____ $:_____
O WISH   O HAVE

'97
$16.5

PRACTICE MAKES PERFECT

ITEM #	INTRO	STATUS	OSRP	GBTRU	NO
68830	1996	CURRENT	$32.50	**$32.50**	CHANGE

Product: Waterglobe, Music Box
Material: Bisque/Glass/Resin
Description: Puffin watches Snowbaby play violin.
Particulars: Tune: "Twinkle, Twinkle, Little Star." Size is 6".

DATE:_____ $:_____
O WISH   O HAVE

'97
$32.5

NOW I LAY ME DOWN TO SLEEP

ITEM #	INTRO	STATUS	OSRP	GBTRU	NO
68831	1996	CURRENT	$32.50	**$32.50**	CHANGE

Product: Waterglobe, Music Box
Material: Bisque/Glass/Resin
Description: Snowbaby says bedtime prayers.
Particulars: Tune: "Brahms' Lullaby." Size is 6".

DATE:_____ $:_____
O WISH   O HAVE

'97
$32.5

ONCE UPON A TIME

ITEM #	INTRO	STATUS	OSRP	GBTRU	NO
68832	1996	CURRENT	$30.00	**$30.00**	CHANGE

Product: Animated Moving Musical
Description: Stack of books with Snowbaby sitting on top reading from a book. Head moves when tune is played.
Particulars: Tune: "When You Wish Upon A Star." Mother's Day 1997 Promotion: Participating Dealers had a Limited Edition Print from the Snowbabies™ Winter Tales Book available for collectors who purchased this piece for Mother's Day.

DATE:_____ $:_____
O WISH   O HAVE

'97
$30

Snowbabies™

Sliding Through The Milky Way

Item #	Intro	Status	OSRP	GBTru	
68833	1996	Current	$37.50	**$37.50**	NO CHANGE

Product: Music Box
Material: Porcelain
Description: Polar bear rides on sled with Snowbaby.
Particulars: Tune: "Twinkle, Twinkle, Little Star."

DATE:_____ $:_____
○ WISH   ○ HAVE

'97
$37.5

You're My Snowbaby

Item #	Intro	Status	OSRP	GBTru	
68834	1996	Current	$15.00	**$15.00**	NO CHANGE

Product: Picture Frame
Material: Porcelain
Description: Snowbaby peeks over top of frame.
Particulars: Size is 3.5" x 5.5". Holds wallet size photo.

DATE:_____ $:_____
○ WISH   ○ HAVE

'97
$15

Moonbeams

Item #	Intro	Status	OSRP	GBTru	
68835	1996	Current	$20.00	**$20.00**	NO CHANGE

Product: Night Light
Material: Porcelain
Description: Snowbaby sits on crescent moon.
Particulars: Size is 5.5". With Auto Photo Cell. Storybook Gift Box.

DATE:_____ $:_____
○ WISH   ○ HAVE

'97
$20

A Little Night Light

Item #	Intro	Status	OSRP	GBTru	
68836	1996	Current	$75.00	**$75.00**	NO CHANGE

Product: Lamp
Material: Bisque base, Paper shade
Description: Three Snowbabies™ carrying candles form base of lamp.
Particulars: Size is 14".

DATE:_____ $:_____
○ WISH   ○ HAVE

'97
$75

Snowbabies™

DISPLAY YOUR FAVORITE SNOWBABY

ITEM #	INTRO	STATUS	OSRP	GBTRU	NO
68837	1996	CURRENT	$45.00	**$45.00**	CHANGE

Product: Lamp
Material: Bisque base, Paper shade
Description: Base of lamp allows display of favorite Snowbaby figurine.
Particulars: Size is 14".

DATE:_____ $:_____
○ WISH   ○ HAVE

'97
$45

SNOWBABY DISPLAY SLED

ITEM #	INTRO	STATUS	OSRP	GBTRU	NO
68838	1996	CURRENT	$45.00	**$45.00**	CHANGE

Product: Accessory
Material: Wood /Aluminum
Description: White "Flexible Flyer" sled with Snowbabies™ written out between runner and sled platform.
Particulars: Size is 19.5" x 5.75" x 4".

DATE:_____ $:_____
○ WISH   ○ HAVE

'97
$45

WISH UPON A FALLING STAR

ITEM #	INTRO	STATUS	OSRP	GBTRU
68839	1997	CURRENT	$75.00	**$75.00**

Product: Figurine
Material: Porcelain
Description: Snowbaby riding polar bear spots falling stars through telescope. Snowbaby with husky pup makes a wish as friends watch the stars.
Particulars: Midyear release. Size is 6".

DATE:_____ $:_____
○ WISH   ○ HAVE

TWO LITTLE BABIES ON THE GO!

ITEM #	INTRO	STATUS	OSRP	GBTRU
68840	1997	CURRENT	$32.50	**$32.50**

Product: Figurine
Material: Porcelain
Description: Two Snowbabies™ ride a metal sled with narrow wood slats.
Particulars: Size is 4". Midyear release.

DATE:_____ $:_____
○ WISH   ○ HAVE

Snowbabies™

Best Little Star

Item #	Intro	Status	OSRP	GBTru
68842	1997	Current	$16.00	**$16.00**

Product: Figurine
Material: Porcelain
Description: Snowbaby wears a star on front of snowsuit.
Particulars: Size is 4.5". Midyear release.

DATE:_____ $:_____
○ WISH   ○ HAVE

Wishing You A Merry Christmas!

Item #	Intro	Status	OSRP	GBTru
68843	1997	Current	$40.00	**$40.00**

Product: Figurine
Material: Porcelain
Description: Two Snowbabies™ hold a Christmas banner to show a polar bear and penguin.
Particulars: Size is 4.25". Midyear release.

DATE:_____ $:_____
○ WISH   ○ HAVE

One, Two, High Button Shoe

Item #	Intro	Status	OSRP	GBTru
68844	1997	Current	$12.50	**$12.50**

Product: Ornament
Material: Porcelain
Description: One Snowbaby is tucked inside as another sits on the toe of an old-fashioned shoe.
Particulars: Bootiebaby ornament. Size is 3.5". Midyear release.

DATE:_____ $:_____
○ WISH   ○ HAVE

Three, Four, No Room For One More

Item #	Intro	Status	OSRP	GBTru
68845	1997	Current	$12.50	**$12.50**

Product: Ornament
Material: Porcelain
Description: Walrus sits in a shoe as Snowbaby holds onto laces from the back of shoe.
Particulars: Bootiebaby ornament. Size is 3". Midyear release.

DATE:_____ $:_____
○ WISH   ○ HAVE

Snowbabies™

SURPRISE

ITEM #	INTRO	STATUS	OSRP	GBTRU
68846	1997	CURRENT	$15.00	**$15.00**

Product: Hinged Box
Material: Porcelain
Description: Two Snowbabies™ pop out of a box.
Particulars: Size is 2.5". Midyear release.

DATE:_____ $:_____
○ WISH   ○ HAVE

CELEBRATE

ITEM #	INTRO	STATUS	OSRP	GBTRU
68847	1997	CURRENT	$15.00	**$15.00**

Product: Hinged Box
Material: Porcelain
Description: Seated Snowbaby plays horn.
Particulars: Size is 3". Midyear release.

DATE:_____ $:_____
○ WISH   ○ HAVE

ROCK-A-BYE BABY

ITEM #	INTRO	STATUS	OSRP	GBTRU
68848	1997	EVENT PIECE	$15.00	**$25.00**

Product: Hinged Box
Material: Porcelain
Description: Winged Snowbaby uses a star to fish for dreams from tiny boat.
Particulars: Special Event piece available December 5 - 7, 1997 to celebrate the 10th Anniversary of Snowbabies™. Dated in gold on the inside.

DATE:_____ $:_____
○ WISH   ◑ HAVE

The Big Snowbabies™ Shake-Up

The news about Snowbabies™ from the 1997 National Stationery Show couldn't have been any more surprising unless Department 56, Inc. had retired the entire line. It certainly caught many people off guard.

Dealers and collectors had known for a month or so that the retirement date for Snowbabies™ had been moved back to December, so to many this was actually old news. But, when you coupled it with the announcement of a Snowbabies™ collectors' club, it was clear that Department 56's intentions were to completely separate the Snowbabies™ from the villages.

(continued page 78)

Snowbabies™

The Big Snowbabies™ Shake-Up (continued from page 77)

Many people think that there was always a distinct separation between the two collectibles lines, but the Snowbabies™, for the most part, were treated as an "also-ran"—not that this was intentional…at least not in a way to cause harm to the sales and collectibility of the product. However, they did suffer by being in the shadow of the villages. When the retirement day for the villages was moved to coincide with the Homes for the Holidays promotions, the Snowbabies™ tagged along. What did the Snowbabies™ have to do with **Homes** for the Holidays? They were destined to stand by and watch the excitement of the day being directed toward the villages. But with this new life, they will be more autonomous, truly competing with other figurines in their price category.

The timing for all this couldn't have been better as Snowbabies™ were celebrating their tenth anniversary. Department 56, Inc. observed this occasion by deeming it the "Snowbabies™ Journey 1987-1997". The "Journey" event was held December 5-7, 1997.

There were three event pieces available at dealers participating in the event. One was the *Rock-A-Bye Baby* Bisque Porcelain Hinged Box. "1997" was painted in gold inside the box. The second event piece was the *Snowbabies™ 1997 Bisque Friendship Pin.* It has "1997" on the back. The third event piece is titled *A Snowbabies™ Journey 1987-1997…Let's Go See Jack Frost.* This piece has a couple of unique aspects to it. First, it has an acrylic base—the first time this has been attempted for a Snowbabies™ piece. Second, it has gold writing on the open pages of the book.

The collectors' club, called the Snowbabies Friendship Club™, features a membership piece, *You'd Better Watch Out!* This club, the first of its kind for Department 56, Inc., will be another factor that will allow the Snowbabies™ line to compete directly with figurines produced by other companies. If you're a Snowbabies™ collector, hopefully you enrolled as a charter member.

Other new pieces introduced in May included *Wish Upon a Falling Star*. This design has two Snowbabies™ and a crowd of animals watching a falling star. *Two Little Babies on the Go!* have to hold on tight as they take a ride on their metal and wood sled. A Snowbaby receives a badge of merit in *Best Little Star.* And, for the first time, the Snowbabies™ themselves will be *Wishing You a Merry Christmas.* This design features two Snowbabies™ unfurling a banner as two friends read the wish "Merry Christmas."

There are also four more ornaments to hang on your Snowbabies™ tree! Two are bisque, and two are mercury glass. The porcelain ones are called *One, Two, High Button Shoe* and *Three, Four, No Room for One More*. These two designs marked the beginning of a new line of Snowbabies™ Bootiebaby ornaments.

The new glass ornaments, like the previous ones, have a glass Snowbaby star and metal Department 56 clock logo hanging from their tops. *Snowbaby on Tree* features a Snowbaby with gold wings holding a gold star and standing atop a green Christmas tree. *Snowbaby on Drum* has a Snowbaby with gold wings playing a concertina and standing atop a drum.

the **Village Chronicle**.

Hinged boxes are a popular introduction for Department 56, Inc., not only in the Snowbabies™ line, but also in various forms of giftware. You already know about the hinged box Snowbabies™ event piece, and there are two more in the regular line. Two Snowbabies™ pop up from inside a gift box in *Surprise*. In *Celebrate*, a Snowbaby sits on a drum while playing a trumpet.

Snowbabies™

SNOWBABIES™ 1997 BISQUE FRIENDSHIP PIN

ITEM #	INTRO	STATUS	OSRP	GBTru
68849	1997	Event Piece	$5.00	**$10.00**

Product: Pin
Material: Porcelain
Description: Snowbaby face on pin.
Particulars: Special Event piece available December 5 - 7, 1997 to celebrate the 10th Anniversary of Snowbabies™. Dated on the back.

DATE:_____ $:_____
○ WISH ● HAVE

CELEBRATING A SNOWBABIES™ JOURNEY, 1987-1998...LET'S GO SEE JACK FROST

ITEM #	INTRO	STATUS	OSRP	GBTru
68850	1997	Event Piece	$60.00	**$75.00**

Product: Figurine
Material: Porcelain/Acrylic
Description: Two Snowbabies™ check a map as polar bear and penguin watch.
Particulars: Special Event piece available December 5 - 7, 1997 to celebrate the 10th Anniversary of Snowbabies™. Acrylic base is a Snowbaby first. Gold accents.

DATE:_____ $:_____
○ WISH ○ HAVE

HEIGH-HO, HEIGH-HO, TO FROLIC LAND WE GO!

ITEM #	INTRO	STATUS	OSRP	GBTru
68853	1997	Current	$48.00	**$48.00**

Product: Figurine
Material: Porcelain
Description: Four Snowbabies™ march to a tune played on a horn while carrying a tree.
Particulars: Size is 4.25".

DATE:_____ $:_____
○ WISH ○ HAVE

WHISTLE WHILE YOU WORK

ITEM #	INTRO	STATUS	OSRP	GBTru
68854	1997	Current	$32.50	**$32.50**

Product: Figurine
Material: Porcelain
Description: Snowbabies™ carry a shoulder-pole balancing a kettle full of stars.
Particulars: Size is 4".

DATE:_____ $:_____
○ WISH ○ HAVE

Snowbabies™

JINGLE BELL

ITEM #	INTRO	STATUS	OSRP	GBTRU
68855	1997	CURRENT	$16.00	**$16.00**

Product: Figurine
Material: Porcelain
Description: Snowbaby rings bell.
Particulars: Size is 4". Gift box.

DATE:_____ $:_____
○ WISH ◉ HAVE

STARLIGHT SERENADE

ITEM #	INTRO	STATUS	OSRP	GBTRU
68856	1997	CURRENT	$25.00	**$25.00**

Product: Figurine
Material: Porcelain
Description: Seated by a tree a Snowbaby plays a mandolin underneath a dangling star.
Particulars: Size is 5.25".

DATE:_____ $:_____
○ WISH ○ HAVE

THANK YOU

ITEM #	INTRO	STATUS	OSRP	GBTRU
68857	1997	CURRENT	$32.50	**$32.50**

Product: Figurine
Material: Porcelain
Description: Snowbaby receives a gift from a friend as they sit by a candle-lit tree.
Particulars: Size is 5.5".

DATE:_____ $:_____
○ WISH ○ HAVE

ONE FOR YOU, ONE FOR ME

ITEM #	INTRO	STATUS	OSRP	GBTRU
68858	1997	CURRENT	$27.50	**$27.50**

Product: Figurine
Material: Porcelain
Description: Snowbabies™ exchange gifts.
Particulars: Size is 4.25".

DATE:_____ $:_____
○ WISH ○ HAVE

Snowbabies™

SHIP O' DREAMS

ITEM #	INTRO	STATUS	OSRP	GBTRU
68859	1997	CURRENT	$135.00	**$135.00**

Product: Figurines
Material: Porcelain
Description: Snowbabies™, bears, puffins and penguins sail the starry sky.
Particulars: Set of 2. Sizes are 10" and 3.25".

DATE:_____ $:_____
○ WISH   ○ HAVE

ALL WE NEED IS LOVE

ITEM #	INTRO	STATUS	OSRP	GBTRU
68860	1997	EVENT PIECE	$32.50	**$32.50**

Product: Figurine
Material: Porcelain
Description: Snowbaby hugs snowman as penguins watch.
Particulars: 1998 Mother's Day Event Piece. Size is 5". Print is available for collectors who purchase piece for Mother's Day.

DATE:_____ $:_____
○ WISH   ○ HAVE

CANDLELIGHT TREES

ITEM #	INTRO	STATUS	OSRP	GBTRU
68861	1997	CURRENT	$25.00	**$25.00**

Product: Accessories
Material: Porcelain
Description: Fir trees decorated with lit candles and a star as a tree-topper.
Particulars: Set of 3. Sizes are 6", 5.5" & 4.5".

DATE:_____ $:_____
○ WISH   ○ HAVE

I'M THE STAR ATOP YOUR TREE!

ITEM #	INTRO	STATUS	OSRP	GBTRU
68862	1997	CURRENT	$20.00	**$20.00**

Product: Tree Topper
Material: Porcelain
Description: Snowbaby carries large star.
Particulars: Size is 7".

DATE:_____ $:_____
○ WISH   ○ HAVE

Snowbabies™

CANDLE LIGHT ... SEASON BRIGHT

ITEM #	INTRO	STATUS	OSRP	GBTru
68863	1997	CURRENT	$20.00	**$20.00**

Product: Tree Topper
Material: Porcelain
Description: Snowbaby and puffins sit at base of candlestick.
Particulars: Size is 7".

DATE:_____ $:_____
○ WISH   ○ HAVE

CANDLE LIGHT ... SEASON BRIGHT

ITEM #	INTRO	STATUS	OSRP	GBTru
68864	1997	CURRENT	$13.50	**$13.50**

Product: Clip-on Ornament
Material: Porcelain
Description: Snowbaby and puffins sit at base of candlestick.
Particulars: Size is 4".

DATE:_____ $:_____
○ WISH   ○ HAVE

FIVE, SIX, A DRUM WITH STICKS

ITEM #	INTRO	STATUS	OSRP	GBTru
68865	1997	CURRENT	$13.50	**$13.50**

Product: Ornament
Material: Porcelain
Description: Snowbaby in a shoe plays drum.
Particulars: Bootiebaby ornament. Size is 4".

DATE:_____ $:_____
○ WISH   ○ HAVE

I LOVE YOU

ITEM #	INTRO	STATUS	OSRP	GBTru
68867	1997	EVENT PIECE	$15.00	**$15.00**

Product: Hinged Box
Material: Porcelain
Description: Snowbaby hugs a small snowman. Base of box spells LOVE.
Particulars: Mother's Day Event Piece. Size is 2.75".

DATE:_____ $:_____
○ WISH   ○ HAVE

Snowbabies™

Thank You for purchasing this GREENBOOK Guide. We'd like to let you know when updates are published and to learn a little bit more about you and how we can help you. Please return this postage-paid card to us and we'll also enter your name in our Quarterly GREENBOOK Guide and Collectible Thank You Giveaway Drawing. We'll be giving away a Guide and a current piece from the Collection covered four times a year...at the end of March, June, September and December. All responses received that quarter will go into the drawing. *Please visit our website at: www.greenbooks.com*

Name:

Complete Street Address:

Town & Zip:

Telephone: _____ Email Address: _____

☐ I own a computer w/CD drive & would like information on GREENBOOK Contemporary Collectible CD Roms.

☐ I purchased/received the <u>GREENBOOK</u> Guide to: *(Check All That Apply)* ☐ Beanie Babies ☐ Boyds Collectibles
☐ Charming Tails ☑ Cherished Teddies by Enesco ☑ Department 56® Villages ☐ Department 56® Snowbabies™
☑ Hallmark Keepsake Ornaments ☐ Hallmark Kiddie Cars ☐ Harbour Lights ☑ Precious Moments Company Dolls
☐ Precious Moments Figurines by Enesco ☐ Walt Disney Classics Collections

I collect: *(Check All That Apply)* ☑ Annalee Dolls ☐ Armani Figurines ☐ Barbie ☐ Beanie Babies ☐ Thomas
Blackshear Sculptures ☐ Boyds Collectibles ☐ Cat's Meow ☐ Charming Tails ☑ Cherished Teddies by Enesco
☐ Christopher Radko Ornaments ☐ Coca Cola Collectibles ☑ Department 56® Villages ☑ Department 56® Snowbabies™
☐ Dreamsicles ☐ Fenton Glass ☐ Greenwich Workshop ☑ Hallmark Keepsake Ornaments ☐ Hallmark Kiddie Cars
☐ Harbour Lights ☐ Harmony Kingdom Collectibles ☐ Hummel Figurines by Goebel ☐ Berta Hummel Collectibles
☐ Emmet Kelly, Jr. ☐ Thomas Kinkade ☐ Sandra Kuck Figurines ☐ Lefton Carousel Collection ☐ LLadro
☐ Precious Moments Company Dolls ☐ Precious Moments Figurines by Enesco ☑ Sarah's Attic ☐ Seraphim
Angels by Roman ☐ Sheila's Collectibles ☐ Steiff ☐ Swarovski Silver Crystal ☐ Walt Disney Classics Collection
☐ Other _Cabbage Patch Dolls, John wayne, Madame Alexander Dolls from the Mint_

BUSINESS REPLY MAIL

FIRST-CLASS MAIL PERMIT 9640 PACIFIC GROVE, CALIFORNIA

POSTAGE WILL BE PAID BY ADDRESSEE

GREENBOOK

Collectors' Information Services
P.O. Box 645
Pacific Grove CA 93950-9989

SWEET DREAMS

ITEM #	INTRO	STATUS	OSRP	GBTRU
68868	1997	CURRENT	$15.00	**$15.00**

Product: Hinged Box
Material: Porcelain
Description: Snowbaby kneels on star-shaped box to say nighttime prayers.
Particulars: Size is 2.5".

DATE:_____ $:_____
○ WISH   ○ HAVE

POLAR EXPRESS

ITEM #	INTRO	STATUS	OSRP	GBTRU
68869	1997	CURRENT	$15.00	**$15.00**

Product: Hinged Box
Material: Porcelain
Description: Snowbaby riding on a polar bear.
Particulars: Size is 2.5".

DATE:_____ $:_____
○ WISH   ○ HAVE

DID HE SEE YOU?

ITEM #	INTRO	STATUS	OSRP	GBTRU
68870	1997	CURRENT	$37.50	**$37.50**

Product: Moving Musical Figurine
Material: Porcelain
Description: Snowman's head moves back and forth as Snowbabies™ giggle and show friends.
Particulars: Tune: "Winter Wonderland." Size is 5.5".

DATE:_____ $:_____
○ WISH   ◉ HAVE

JINGLE BELL

ITEM #	INTRO	STATUS	OSRP	GBTRU
68871	1997	CURRENT	$32.50	**$32.50**

Product: Waterglobe, Music Box
Material: Bisque/Glass/Resin
Description: Penguins watch Snowbaby ring bell.
Particulars: Tune: "Jingle Bells." Size is 5".

DATE:_____ $:_____
○ WISH   ○ HAVE

Snowbabies™

Heigh-Ho

Item #	Intro	Status	OSRP	GBTru
68872	1997	Current	$32.50	**$32.50**

Product: Waterglobe, Music Box
Material: Bisque/Glass/Resin
Description: Three Snowbabies™ march to a tune on a horn while carrying a tree.
Particulars: Tune: "Heigh-Ho." Size is 5".

DATE:_____ $:_____
○ WISH   ○ HAVE

Moon Beams

Item #	Intro	Status	OSRP	GBTru
68873	1997	Current	$32.50	**$32.50**

Product: Waterglobe, Music Box
Material: Bisque/Glass/Resin
Description: Seated Snowbaby on crescent moon.
Particulars: Tune: "Rock-A-Bye Baby." Size is 5".

DATE:_____ $:_____
○ WISH   ○ HAVE

Snowbabies™ Shelf Unit

Item #	Intro	Status	OSRP	GBTru
68874	1997	Current	$20.00	**$20.00**

Product: Accessory
Material: Wood
Description: Base of shelf is sprinkled with stars and Snowbabies™ is spelled out.
Particulars: Size is 24" x 4.5".

DATE:_____ $:_____
○ WISH   ○ HAVE

Notes: _____

_____

_____

_____

_____

_____

Retired

Item #	Retired	
7601-5	1994	Give Me A Push!
7603-1	1994	Don't Fall Off!
7604-0	1994	Best Friends
7605-8	1992	Are All These Mine?
7607-4	1994	Winter Surprise!
7608-2	1992	Helpful Friends
7609-0	1992	Polar Express
7610-4	1992	Icy Igloo W/Tree
7611-2	1997	Frosty Fun
7613-9	1993	Frosty Frolic
7614-7	1992	Tumbling In The Snow!
7615-5	1993	Tiny Trio
7616-3	1993	Penguin Parade
7617-1	1993	All Fall Down
7618-0	1992	Finding Fallen Stars
7621-0	1993	Twinkle Little Stars
7622-8	1997	Read Me A Story!
7623-6	1993	Playing Games Is Fun!
7624-4	1993	A Special Delivery
7626-0	1995	Wishing On A Star
7627-9	1996	I'll Put Up The Tree!
7628-7	1994	I Made This Just For You!
7629-5	1993	Waiting For Christmas
7630-9	1993	Dancing To A Tune
7631-7	1993	Is That For Me?
7637-6	1996	You Can't Find Me!
7638-4	1997	Help Me, I'm Stuck!
7639-2	1995	This Will Cheer You Up
7640-6	1997	I Need A Hug
7641-4	1995	Wait For Me!
7643-0	1995	You Didn't Forget Me!
7645-7	1995	Join The Parade
7652-0	1997	We Make A Great Pair
7656-2	1997	Somewhere In Dreamland
7661-9	1997	There's Another One
7662-7	1997	I'm Right Behind You
7663-5	1997	We'll Plant The Starry Pines
7666-0	1997	Bringing Starry Pines
7667-8	1997	Lift Me Higher, I Can't Reach!
76691	1997	Are You On My List?

Hold On Tight!

Item #	Intro	Status	OSRP	GBTru	NO
7600-7	1989	Current	$7.00	**$7.00**	CHANGE

Product: Miniature
Material: Pewter
Description: Snowbaby lying on a sled.
Particulars: Size is 1.5".

DATE:_____ $:_____

		'91	'92	'93	'94	'95	'97
○ WISH	○ HAVE	$7	7	7	7	7	7

Give Me A Push!

Item #	Intro	Status	OSRP	GBTru	NO
7601-5	1989	Retired 1994	$7.00	**$14.00**	CHANGE

Product: Miniature
Material: Pewter
Description: Snowbaby with open arms seated on sled.
Particulars: Size is 1.5".

DATE:_____ $:_____

		'91	'92	'93	'94	'95	'97
○ WISH	○ HAVE	$7	7	7	7	12	14

I'm Making Snowballs!

Item #	Intro	Status	OSRP	GBTru	NO
7602-3	1989	Current	$7.00	**$7.00**	CHANGE

Product: Miniature
Material: Pewter
Description: Snowbaby pushing giant snowball.
Particulars: Size is 1.5".

DATE:_____ $:_____

		'91	'92	'93	'94	'95	'97
○ WISH	● HAVE	$7	7	7	7	7	7

Don't Fall Off!

Item #	Intro	Status	OSRP	GBTru	↑
7603-1	1989	Retired 1994	$7.00	**$18.00**	13%

Product: Miniature
Material: Pewter
Description: Snowbaby sitting on a snowball.
Particulars: Size is 1.5".

DATE:_____ $:_____

		'91	'92	'93	'94	'95	'97
○ WISH	○ HAVE	$7	7	7	7	12	16

Snowbabies™ Miniatures

BEST FRIENDS

Item #	Intro	Status	OSRP	GBTru	↑
7604-0	1989	Retired 1994	$10.00	**$20.00**	11%

Product: Miniature
Material: Pewter
Description: Snowbabies™ put arms around each other.
Particulars: Size is 1.5".

DATE:	$:	'91	'92	'93	'94	'95	'97
○ WISH ○ HAVE		$10	10	10	10	18	18

ARE ALL THESE MINE?

Item #	Intro	Status	OSRP	GBTru	↓
7605-8	1989	Retired 1992	$7.00	**$16.00**	20%

Product: Miniature
Material: Pewter
Description: Snowbaby holds stocking full of stars.
Particulars: Size is 1.5".

DATE:	$:	'91	'92	'93	'94	'95	'97
○ WISH ○ HAVE		$7	7	16	22	18	20

DOWN THE HILL WE GO!

Item #	Intro	Status	OSRP	GBTru	NO
7606-6	1989	Current	$13.50	**$13.50**	CHANGE

Product: Miniatures
Material: Pewter
Description: Two Snowbabies™ on toboggan.
Particulars: Set of 2. Size is 1".

DATE:	$:	'91	'92	'93	'94	'95	'97
○ WISH ● HAVE		$13.5	13.5	13.5	13.5	13.5	13.5

WINTER SURPRISE!

Item #	Intro	Status	OSRP	GBTru	↑
7607-4	1989	Retired 1994	$13.50	**$24.00**	20%

Product: Miniature
Material: Pewter
Description: Two Snowbabies™ peek out of gift box.
Particulars: Size is 1".

DATE:	$:	'91	'92	'93	'94	'95	'97
○ WISH ● HAVE		$13.5	13.5	13.5	13.5	20	20

Snowbabies™ Miniatures

HELPFUL FRIENDS

ITEM #	INTRO	STATUS	OSRP	GBTRU	NO
7608-2	1989	RETIRED 1992	$13.50	**$30.00**	CHANGE

Product: Miniatures
Material: Pewter
Description: Snowbaby and penguins with box of stars.
Particulars: Set of 4. Sizes range from 1" to 1.5".

DATE:_____	$:_____	'91	'92	'93	'94	'95	'97
○ WISH	○ HAVE	$13.5	13.5	24	30	30	30

POLAR EXPRESS

ITEM #	INTRO	STATUS	OSRP	GBTRU	NO
7609-0	1989	RETIRED 1992	$13.50	**$30.00**	CHANGE

Product: Miniatures
Material: Pewter
Description: Two Snowbabies™ ride on a polar bear.
Particulars: Set of 2. Size is 2.5".

DATE:_____	$:_____	'91	'92	'93	'94	'95	'97
○ WISH	○ HAVE	$13.5	13.5	30	35	25	30

ICY IGLOO W/TREE

ITEM #	INTRO	STATUS	OSRP	GBTRU	↑
7610-4	1989	RETIRED 1992	$7.50	**$25.00**	4%

Product: Miniature Accessories
Material: Pewter
Description: Snow house.
Particulars: Set of 2. Size is 2".

DATE:_____	$:_____	'91	'92	'93	'94	'95	'97
○ WISH	○ HAVE	$7.5	7.5	15	22	22	24

FROSTY FUN

ITEM #	INTRO	STATUS	OSRP	GBTRU	↑
7611-2	1989	RETIRED 1997	$13.50	**$28.00**	107%

Product: Miniatures
Material: Pewter
Description: Snowbabies™ build a snowman.
Particulars: Set of 2. Size is 1.5".

DATE:_____	$:_____	'91	'92	'93	'94	'95	'97
○ WISH	○ HAVE	$13.5	13.5	13.5	13.5	13.5	13.5

Snowbabies™ Miniatures

FROSTY FOREST

Item #	Intro	Status	OSRP	GBTru	NO
7612-0	1989	Current	$12.00	**$12.00**	CHANGE

Product: Miniature Accessories
Material: Pewter
Description: Two evergreens.
Particulars: Set of 2. Sizes are 2" and 1.5".

DATE:_____ $:_____		'91	'92	'93	'94	'95	'97
○ WISH	○ HAVE	$12	12	12	12	12	12

FROSTY FROLIC

Item #	Intro	Status	OSRP	GBTru	↑
7613-9	1989	Retired 1993	$24.00	**$35.00**	17%

Product: Miniatures
Material: Pewter
Description: Snowbabies™ hold hands and circle tree.
Particulars: Set of 4. Sizes are 1.5" to 2.5".

DATE:_____ $:_____		'91	'92	'93	'94	'95	'97
○ WISH	○ HAVE	$24	24	24	38	30	30

TUMBLING IN THE SNOW!

Item #	Intro	Status	OSRP	GBTru	↓
7614-7	1989	Retired 1992	$30.00	**$60.00**	20%

Product: Miniatures
Material: Pewter
Description: Snowbabies™ tumbling in the snow.
Particulars: Set of 5. Sizes range from 1" to 1.5".

DATE:_____ $:_____		'91	'92	'93	'94	'95	'97
○ WISH	○ HAVE	$30	30	80	74	75	75

TINY TRIO

Item #	Intro	Status	OSRP	GBTru	↑
7615-5	1989	Retired 1993	$18.00	**$32.00**	7%

Product: Miniatures
Material: Pewter
Description: Snowbaby band.
Particulars: Set of 3. Sizes range from 1.25" to 1.5".

DATE:_____ $:_____		'91	'92	'93	'94	'95	'97
○ WISH	● HAVE	$18	18	18	32	35	30

Snowbabies™ Miniatures

PENGUIN PARADE

ITEM #	INTRO	STATUS	OSRP	GBTRU	↑
7616-3	1989	RETIRED 1993	$12.50	**$33.00**	10%

Product: Miniatures
Material: Pewter
Description: Penguins follow Snowbaby playing flute.
Particulars: Set of 4. Sizes range from .75" to 1.5".

DATE:_____	$:_____	'91	'92	'93	'94	'95	'97
○ WISH	○ HAVE	$12.5	12.5	12.5	28	28	30

ALL FALL DOWN

ITEM #	INTRO	STATUS	OSRP	GBTRU	↑
7617-1	1989	RETIRED 1993	$25.00	**$44.00**	5%

Product: Miniatures
Material: Pewter
Description: Ice-skating Snowbabies™ fall down.
Particulars: Set of 4. Size is 1.5".

DATE:_____	$:_____	'91	'92	'93	'94	'95	'97
○ WISH	○ HAVE	$25	25	25	35	35	42

FINDING FALLEN STARS

ITEM #	INTRO	STATUS	OSRP	GBTRU	↑
7618-0	1989	RETIRED 1992	$12.50	**$40.00**	25%

Product: Miniatures
Material: Pewter
Description: Snowbabies™ collect fallen stars in a basket.
Particulars: Set of 2. Size is 1.5".

DATE:_____	$:_____	'91	'92	'93	'94	'95	'97
○ WISH	○ HAVE	$12.5	12.5	35	35	25	32

FROSTY FROLIC LAND

ITEM #	INTRO	STATUS	OSRP	GBTRU	NO
7619-8	1989	CURRENT	$96.00	**$96.00**	CHANGE

Product: Miniature Accessories
Material: Resin & Sisal
Description: Landscape.
Particulars: Set of 3. Size is 16" x 8".

DATE:_____	$:_____	'91	'92	'93	'94	'95	'97
○ WISH	○ HAVE	$96	96	96	96	96	96

Snowbabies™ Miniatures

COLLECTOR'S SIGN

ITEM #	INTRO	STATUS	OSRP	GBTRU	NO
7620-1	1989	CURRENT	$7.00	**$7.00**	CHANGE

Product: Miniature Accessory
Material: Pewter
Description: Collector's sign.
Particulars: Size is 1.5".

DATE:_____ $:_____	'91	'92	'93	'94	'95	'97
○ WISH ○ HAVE	$7	7	7	7	7	7

TWINKLE LITTLE STARS

ITEM #	INTRO	STATUS	OSRP	GBTRU	↑
7621-0	1990	RETIRED 1993	$15.00	**$30.00**	7%

Product: Miniatures
Material: Pewter
Description: Three Snowbabies™ sing carols.
Particulars: Set of 2. Size is 1.25".

DATE:_____ $:_____	'91	'92	'93	'94	'95	'97
○ WISH ○ HAVE	$15	15	15	28	28	28

READ ME A STORY!

ITEM #	INTRO	STATUS	OSRP	GBTRU	↑
7622-8	1990	RETIRED 1997	$11.00	**$17.00**	55%

Product: Miniature
Material: Pewter
Description: Snowbaby reads story to penguins.
Particulars: Size is 1.25".

DATE:_____ $:_____	'91	'92	'93	'94	'95	'97
○ WISH ○ HAVE	$11	11	11	11	11	11

PLAYING GAMES IS FUN!

ITEM #	INTRO	STATUS	OSRP	GBTRU	NO
7623-6	1990	RETIRED 1993	$13.50	**$28.00**	CHANGE

Product: Miniatures
Material: Pewter
Description: Snowbabies™ play London Bridge with penguins.
Particulars: Set of 2. Size is 1.25".

DATE:_____ $:_____	'91	'92	'93	'94	'95	'97
○ WISH ○ HAVE	$13.5	13.5	13.5	22	20	28

Snowbabies™ Miniatures

1990...

A Special Delivery

Item #	Intro	Status	OSRP	GBTru	NO
7624-4	1990	Retired 1993	$7.00	**$18.00**	CHANGE

Product: Miniature
Material: Pewter
Description: Snowbaby on snowshoes delivers star.
Particulars: Size is 1.25".

DATE:____	$:____	'91	'92	'93	'94	'95	'97
○ WISH	○ HAVE	$7	7	7	14	15	18

Why Don't You Talk To Me?

Item #	Intro	Status	OSRP	GBTru	NO
7625-2	1991	Current	$12.00	**$12.00**	CHANGE

Product: Miniatures
Material: Pewter
Description: Snowbaby asks snowman a question.
Particulars: Set of 2. Size is 1.5".

DATE:____	$:____	'91	'92	'93	'94	'95	'97
○ WISH	○ HAVE	$12	12	12	12	12	12

Wishing On A Star

Item #	Intro	Status	OSRP	GBTru	NO
7626-0	1991	Retired 1995	$10.00	**$25.00**	CHANGE

Product: Miniature
Material: Pewter
Description: Penguin watches Snowbaby holding up star
to wish upon.
Particulars: Size is 1.25".

DATE:____	$:____	'91	'92	'93	'94	'95	'97
○ WISH	○ HAVE	$10	10	10	10	10	25

I'll Put Up The Tree!

Item #	Intro	Status	OSRP	GBTru	↑
7627-9	1991	Retired 1996	$9.00	**$20.00**	82%

Product: Miniature
Material: Pewter
Description: Snowbaby holds small tree with star.
Particulars: Size is 1.25".

DATE:____	$:____	'91	'92	'93	'94	'95	'97
○ WISH	○ HAVE	$9	9	9	9	9	11

Snowbabies™ Miniatures

I MADE THIS JUST FOR YOU!

ITEM #	INTRO	STATUS	OSRP	GBTRU	NO
7628-7	1991	RETIRED 1994	$7.00	**$18.00**	CHANGE

Product: Miniature
Material: Pewter
Description: Snowbaby carrying a star wreath.
Particulars: Size is 1.25".

		'92	'93	'94	'95	'97
DATE:_____ $:_____		$7	7	7	11	18
○ WISH ○ HAVE						

WAITING FOR CHRISTMAS

ITEM #	INTRO	STATUS	OSRP	GBTRU	NO
7629-5	1991	RETIRED 1993	$12.50	**$22.00**	CHANGE

Product: Miniature
Material: Pewter
Description: Two Snowbabies™ sitting on opposite sides of gift–one watches, one naps.
Particulars: Size is 1.25".

		'92	'93	'94	'95	'97
DATE:_____ $:_____		$12.5	12.5	22	20	22
○ WISH ○ HAVE						

DANCING TO A TUNE

ITEM #	INTRO	STATUS	OSRP	GBTRU	↓
7630-9	1991	RETIRED 1993	$18.00	**$25.00**	17%

Product: Miniatures
Material: Pewter
Description: Snowbaby plays concertina as two Snowbabies™ dance.
Particulars: Set of 3. Size is 1.5".

		'92	'93	'94	'95	'97
DATE:_____ $:_____		$18	18	32	25	30
○ WISH ○ HAVE						

IS THAT FOR ME?

ITEM #	INTRO	STATUS	OSRP	GBTRU	NO
7631-7	1991	RETIRED 1993	$12.50	**$22.00**	CHANGE

Product: Miniatures
Material: Pewter
Description: One Snowbaby holds gift for another.
Particulars: Set of 2. Size is 1.5".

		'92	'93	'94	'95	'97
DATE:_____ $:_____		$12.5	12.5	18	18	22
○ WISH ○ HAVE						

Snowbabies™ Miniatures

1992...

LET'S GO SKIING

ITEM #	INTRO	STATUS	OSRP	GBT$_{RU}$	NO
7636-8	1992	CURRENT	$7.00	**$7.00**	CHANGE

Product: Miniature
Material: Pewter
Description: Snowbaby holds skis.
Particulars: Size is 1.5".

DATE:_____	$:_____		'93	'94	'95	'97
○ WISH	● HAVE		$7	7	7	7

YOU CAN'T FIND ME!

ITEM #	INTRO	STATUS	OSRP	GBT$_{RU}$	↑
7637-6	1992	RETIRED 1996	$22.50	**$32.00**	28%

Product: Miniatures
Material: Pewter
Description: Snowbabies™ with penguins playing hide-and-seek.
Particulars: Set of 4. Size is 1.5".

DATE:_____	$:_____		'93	'94	'95	'97
○ WISH	○ HAVE		$22.5	22.5	22.5	25

HELP ME, I'M STUCK!

ITEM #	INTRO	STATUS	OSRP	GBT$_{RU}$	↑
7638-4	1992	RETIRED 1997	$15.00	**$20.00**	33%

Product: Miniatures
Material: Pewter
Description: Snowbaby under pile of stars gets helping hand.
Particulars: Set of 2. Size is 1.5".

DATE:_____	$:_____		'93	'94	'95	'97
○ WISH	○ HAVE		$15	15	15	15

THIS WILL CHEER YOU UP

ITEM #	INTRO	STATUS	OSRP	GBT$_{RU}$	↑
7639-2	1992	RETIRED 1995	$13.75	**$20.00**	33%

Product: Miniature
Material: Pewter
Description: Snowbabies™ exchanging star.
Particulars: Size is 1.5".

DATE:_____	$:_____		'93	'94	'95	'97
○ WISH	○ HAVE		$13.75	13.75	13.75	15

Snowbabies™ Miniatures

I NEED A HUG

ITEM #	INTRO	STATUS	OSRP	GBTRU	↑
7640-6	1992	RETIRED 1997	$10.00	**$15.00**	50%

Product: Miniature
Material: Pewter
Description: Two Snowbabies™ hug.
Particulars: Size is 1.5".

DATE:_____ $:_____
○ WISH ● HAVE

'93	'94	'95	'97
$10	10	10	10

WAIT FOR ME!

ITEM #	INTRO	STATUS	OSRP	GBTRU	↑
7641-4	1992	RETIRED 1995	$22.50	**$30.00**	25%

Product: Miniatures
Material: Pewter
Description: Snowbaby pushes sled filled with presents and stars as two penguins follow.
Particulars: Set of 4. Size is 3".

DATE:_____ $:_____
○ WISH ○ HAVE

'93	'94	'95	'97
$22.5	22.5	22.5	24

SHALL I PLAY FOR YOU?

ITEM #	INTRO	STATUS	OSRP	GBTRU	NO
7642-2	1992	CURRENT	$7.00	**$7.00**	CHANGE

Product: Miniature
Material: Pewter
Description: Snowbaby playing drum.
Particulars: Size is 1.5".

DATE:_____ $:_____
○ WISH ○ HAVE

'93	'94	'95	'97
$7	7	7	7

YOU DIDN'T FORGET ME!

ITEM #	INTRO	STATUS	OSRP	GBTRU	↑
7643-0	1992	RETIRED 1995	$17.50	**$25.00**	32%

Product: Miniatures
Material: Pewter
Description: Snowbaby getting mail.
Particulars: Set of 3. Size is 1.5".

DATE:_____ $:_____
○ WISH ● HAVE

'93	'94	'95	'97
$17.5	17.5	17.5	19

Snowbabies™ Miniatures

JUST ONE LITTLE CANDLE

ITEM #	INTRO	STATUS	OSRP	GBTRU	NO
7644-9	1992	CURRENT	$7.00	**$7.00**	CHANGE

Product: Miniature
Material: Pewter
Description: Snowbaby holding candle.
Particulars: Size is 1.5".

DATE:_____ $:_____

		'93	'94	'95	'97
○ WISH	○ HAVE	$7	7	7	7

JOIN THE PARADE

ITEM #	INTRO	STATUS	OSRP	GBTRU	↑
7645-7	1992	RETIRED 1995	$22.50	**$28.00**	17%

Product: Miniatures
Material: Pewter
Description: Snowbaby marching with friends.
Particulars: Set of 4. Size is 3".

DATE:_____ $:_____

		'93	'94	'95	'97
○ WISH	○ HAVE	$22.5	22.5	22.5	24

WE MAKE A GREAT PAIR

ITEM #	INTRO	STATUS	OSRP	GBTRU	↑
7652-0	1993	RETIRED 1997	$13.50	**$18.00**	33%

Product: Miniature
Material: Pewter
Description: Snowbaby friends ice skating.
Particulars: Size is 1.5".

DATE:_____ $:_____

		'94	'95	'97
○ WISH	○ HAVE	$13.5	13.5	13.5

WILL IT SNOW TODAY?

ITEM #	INTRO	STATUS	OSRP	GBTRU	NO
7653-8	1993	CURRENT	$22.50	**$22.50**	CHANGE

Product: Miniatures
Material: Pewter
Description: Snowbaby, penguin, and walrus check weather vane for forecast.
Particulars: Set of 5. Size is 3.5".

DATE:_____ $:_____

		'94	'95	'97
○ WISH	○ HAVE	$22.5	22.5	22.5

WHERE DID HE GO?

ITEM #	INTRO	STATUS	OSRP	GBTRU	NO
7654-6	1993	CURRENT	$20.00	**$20.00**	CHANGE

Product: Miniatures
Material: Pewter
Description: Snowbabies™ and penguin check melting snowman.
Particulars: Set of 4. Size is 1.75".

DATE:_____ $:_____
○ WISH   ○ HAVE

'94	'95	'97
$20	20	20

LET'S ALL CHIME IN!

ITEM #	INTRO	STATUS	OSRP	GBTRU	NO
7655-4	1993	CURRENT	$20.00	**$20.00**	CHANGE

Product: Miniatures
Material: Pewter
Description: Three Snowbabies™ as bell ringers.
Particulars: Set of 2. Size is 1.75".

DATE:_____ $:_____
○ WISH   ○ HAVE

'94	'95	'97
$20	20	20

SOMEWHERE IN DREAMLAND

ITEM #	INTRO	STATUS	OSRP	GBTRU	↑
7656-2	1993	RETIRED 1997	$30.00	**$40.00**	33%

Product: Miniatures
Material: Pewter
Description: Snowbabies™ nap on moon watched by bear, puffin and penguin.
Particulars: Set of 5. Size is 3".

DATE:_____ $:_____
○ WISH   ○ HAVE

'94	'95	'97
$30	30	30

NOW I LAY ME DOWN TO SLEEP

ITEM #	INTRO	STATUS	OSRP	GBTRU	NO
7657-0	1993	CURRENT	$7.00	**$7.00**	CHANGE

Product: Miniature
Material: Pewter
Description: Snowbaby says bedtime prayers.
Particulars: Size is 1.25".

DATE:_____ $:_____
○ WISH   ○ HAVE

'94	'95	'97
$7	7	7

Snowbabies™ Miniatures

1993...

WINKEN, BLINKEN, & NOD

ITEM #	INTRO	STATUS	OSRP	GBTRU	NO
7658-9	1993	CURRENT	$27.50	**$27.50**	CHANGE

Product: Miniatures
Material: Pewter
Description: Three Snowbabies™ in star trimmed boat with waves lapping at base. One Snowbaby and penguin scan the horizon. One Snowbaby naps at rear of boat. Middle Snowbaby holds stars.
Particulars: Set of 3. Size is 2".

DATE:_____ $:_____		'94	'95	'97
○ WISH ○ HAVE		$27.5	27.5	27.5

THERE'S ANOTHER ONE

ITEM #	INTRO	STATUS	OSRP	GBTRU	↑
7661-9	1994	RETIRED 1997	$10.00	**$15.00**	50%

Product: Miniature
Material: Pewter
Description: Snowbaby pushing wheelbarrow collecting stars.
Particulars: Size is 1.5".

DATE:_____ $:_____	'95	'97
○ WISH ○ HAVE	$10	10

I'M RIGHT BEHIND YOU

ITEM #	INTRO	STATUS	OSRP	GBTRU	↑
7662-7	1994	RETIRED 1997	$27.50	**$35.00**	27%

Product: Miniatures
Material: Pewter
Description: Snowbabies™ on skates push Snowbabies™ on sled.
Particulars: Set of 5. Size is 1.75".

DATE:_____ $:_____	'95	'97
○ WISH ○ HAVE	$27.5	27.5

WE'LL PLANT THE STARRY PINES

ITEM #	INTRO	STATUS	OSRP	GBTRU	↑
7663-5	1994	RETIRED 1997	$22.00	**$28.00**	27%

Product: Miniatures
Material: Pewter
Description: Snowbabies™ plant tree as another holds next tree.
Particulars: Set of 4. Size is 1.5".

DATE:_____ $:_____	'95	'97
○ WISH ○ HAVE	$22	22

Snowbabies™ Miniatures

Let's Go Skating

Item #	Intro	Status	OSRP	GBTru	NO
7664-3	1994	Current	$7.00	**$7.00**	CHANGE

Product: Miniature
Material: Pewter
Description: Snowbaby holding ice skates in hands.
Particulars: Size is 1.5".

DATE:_____ $:_____	'95	'97
○ WISH ● HAVE	$7	7

Stringing Fallen Stars

Item #	Intro	Status	OSRP	GBTru	NO
7665-1	1994	Current	$8.00	**$8.00**	CHANGE

Product: Miniature
Material: Pewter
Description: Snowbaby strings stars from a box.
Particulars: Size is 1.5".

DATE:_____ $:_____	'95	'97
○ WISH ○ HAVE	$8	8

Bringing Starry Pines

Item #	Intro	Status	OSRP	GBTru	↑
7666-0	1994	Retired 1997	$18.00	**$22.00**	22%

Product: Miniatures
Material: Pewter
Description: Snowbaby pulls a sled loaded with three small pines.
Particulars: Set of 2. Size is 1.5".

DATE:_____ $:_____	'95	'97
○ WISH ○ HAVE	$18	18

Lift Me Higher, I Can't Reach!

Item #	Intro	Status	OSRP	GBTru	↑
7667-8	1994	Retired 1997	$25.00	**$30.00**	20%

Product: Miniatures
Material: Pewter
Description: One Snowbaby lifts another to place a star on a tree. Bear cub and penguin watch trimming.
Particulars: Set of 5. Size is 3".

DATE:_____ $:_____	'95	'97
○ WISH ○ HAVE	$25	25

Snowbabies™ Miniatures

1995...

I Found The Biggest Star Of All

Item #	Intro	Status	OSRP	GBTru	NO
76690	1995	Current	$7.00	**$7.00**	CHANGE

Product: Miniature
Material: Pewter
Description: Snowbaby holds up large star.
Particulars: Size is 1.5".

DATE:_____ $:_____
○ WISH ○ HAVE

'97
$7

Are You On My List?

Item #	Intro	Status	OSRP	GBTru	↑
76691	1995	Retired 1997	$9.00	**$14.00**	56%

Product: Miniatures
Material: Pewter
Description: Snowbaby checks list as puffin watches.
Particulars: Set of 2. Size is 1.5".

DATE:_____ $:_____
○ WISH ○ HAVE

'97
$9

Ring The Bells ... It's Christmas!

Item #	Intro	Status	OSRP	GBTru	NO
76692	1995	Current	$20.00	**$20.00**	CHANGE

Product: Miniature
Material: Pewter
Description: Snowbabies™ pull bell cord to make bell ring.
Particulars: Size is 2.75".

DATE:_____ $:_____
○ WISH ○ HAVE

'97
$20

What Shall We Do Today?

Item #	Intro	Status	OSRP	GBTru	NO
76693	1995	Current	$17.00	**$17.00**	CHANGE

Product: Miniatures
Material: Pewter
Description: Snowbaby leans on wall and discusses plans for the day with penguins.
Particulars: Set of 2.

DATE:_____ $:_____
○ WISH ○ HAVE

'97
$17

Snowbabies™ Miniatures

I See You!

Item #	Intro	Status	OSRP	GBTru	NO
76694	1995	Current	$13.50	**$13.50**	CHANGE

Product: Miniatures
Material: Pewter
Description: Snowbaby peers through telescope and sees star.
Particulars: Set of 2. Size is 1.75".

DATE:_____ $:_____
O WISH   O HAVE

'97
$13.5

I Can't Find Him!

Item #	Intro	Status	OSRP	GBTru	NO
76695	1995	Current	$18.00	**$18.00**	CHANGE

Product: Miniatures
Material: Pewter
Description: One Snowbaby peeks into ice hole to spy on walrus. Second baby finds walrus behind them watching their activity.
Particulars: Set of 3. Size is 2.25".

DATE:_____ $:_____
O WISH   O HAVE

'97
$18

I'll Play A Christmas Tune

Item #	Intro	Status	OSRP	GBTru	NO
76696	1995	Current	$7.50	**$7.50**	CHANGE

Product: Miniature
Material: Pewter
Description: Seated on a toy drum, a Snowbaby plays the piccolo.
Particulars: Size is 1.75".

DATE:_____ $:_____
O WISH   O HAVE

'97
$7.5

We're Building An Icy Igloo

Item #	Intro	Status	OSRP	GBTru	NO
76697	1995	Current	$27.50	**$27.50**	CHANGE

Product: Miniatures
Material: Pewter
Description: Polar bear watches as Snowbabies™ put in place the last ice blocks on igloo.
Particulars: Set of 3. Size is 3.25".

DATE:_____ $:_____
O WISH   O HAVE

'97
$27.5

Snowbabies™ Miniatures

1995...

A STAR-IN-THE-BOX

ITEM #	INTRO	STATUS	OSRP	GBTRU	NO
76698	1995	CURRENT	$7.50	**$7.50**	CHANGE

Product: Miniature
Material: Pewter
Description: Snowbaby as jack-in-the-box, pops out holding up stars.
Particulars: Size is 2".

DATE:_____ $:_____
○ WISH   ○ HAVE

'97
$7.5

MUSH!

ITEM #	INTRO	STATUS	OSRP	GBTRU	NO
76699	1995	CURRENT	$25.00	**$25.00**	CHANGE

Product: Miniatures
Material: Pewter
Description: Snowbabies™ in sleigh give 'go' command to Husky pups.
Particulars: Set of 2. Size is 4.25" x 1.75".

DATE:_____ $:_____
○ WISH   ○ HAVE

'97
$25

I'M SO SLEEPY

ITEM #	INTRO	STATUS	OSRP	GBTRU	NO
76700	1996	CURRENT	$7.00	**$7.00**	CHANGE

Product: Miniature
Material: Pewter
Description: Snowbaby with blanket.
Particulars: Size is 1".

DATE:_____ $:_____
○ WISH   ○ HAVE

'97
$7

WHICH WAY'S UP?

ITEM #	INTRO	STATUS	OSRP	GBTRU	NO
76701	1996	CURRENT	$13.50	**$13.50**	CHANGE

Product: Miniatures
Material: Pewter
Description: Snowbaby standing on head.
Particulars: Set of 2. Size is 1.5".

DATE:_____ $:_____
○ WISH   ○ HAVE

'97
$13.5

Snowbabies™ Miniatures

CLIMB EVERY MOUNTAIN

ITEM #	INTRO	STATUS	OSRP	GBTRU	NO
76702	1996	CURRENT	$27.50	**$27.50**	CHANGE

Product: Miniatures
Material: Pewter
Description: Snowbabies™ climbing a mountain.
Particulars: Set of 5.

DATE:_____ $:_____
○ WISH   ○ HAVE

'97
$27.5

YOU ARE MY LUCKY STAR

ITEM #	INTRO	STATUS	OSRP	GBTRU	NO
76703	1996	CURRENT	$20.00	**$20.00**	CHANGE

Product: Miniatures
Material: Pewter
Description: Snowbaby plays violin as friends listen.
Particulars: Set of 2.

DATE:_____ $:_____
○ WISH   ○ HAVE

'97
$20

WITH HUGS & KISSES

ITEM #	INTRO	STATUS	OSRP	GBTRU	NO
76704	1996	CURRENT	$15.00	**$15.00**	CHANGE

Product: Miniatures
Material: Pewter
Description: Snowbaby with mailbag delivers stars.
Particulars: Set of 2. Size is 1.5".

DATE:_____ $:_____
○ WISH   ○ HAVE

'97
$15

IT'S A GRAND OLD FLAG

ITEM #	INTRO	STATUS	OSRP	GBTRU	NO
76705	1996	CURRENT	$11.00	**$11.00**	CHANGE

Product: Miniature
Material: Pewter
Description: Penguin watches Snowbaby carrying flag.
Particulars: Set of 2. Size is 2.25".

DATE:_____ $:_____
○ WISH   ○ HAVE

'97
$11

Snowbabies™ Miniatures

IT'S SNOWING!

ITEM #	INTRO	STATUS	OSRP	GBTRU	NO
76706	1996	CURRENT	$7.00	**$7.00**	CHANGE

Product: Miniature
Material: Pewter
Description: Snowbaby balances snowflake on foot.
Particulars: Size is 1.5".

DATE:_____ $:_____
○ WISH ○ HAVE

'97
$7

WHEN THE BOUGH BREAKS

ITEM #	INTRO	STATUS	OSRP	GBTRU	NO
76707	1996	CURRENT	$18.00	**$18.00**	CHANGE

Product: Miniature
Material: Pewter
Description: Snowbaby on swing suspended between two pine trees.
Particulars: Size is 2.25".

DATE:_____ $:_____
○ WISH ● HAVE

'97
$18

THERE'S NO PLACE LIKE HOME

ITEM #	INTRO	STATUS	OSRP	GBTRU	NO
76708	1996	CURRENT	$7.50	**$7.50**	CHANGE

Product: Miniature
Material: Pewter
Description: Snowbaby carries star package on a pole.
Particulars: Size is 1.5".

DATE:_____ $:_____
○ WISH ○ HAVE

'97
$7.5

YOU NEED WINGS TOO!

ITEM #	INTRO	STATUS	OSRP	GBTRU	NO
76709	1996	CURRENT	$11.00	**$11.00**	CHANGE

Product: Miniatures
Material: Pewter
Description: Snowbaby attaches wings on a snowman.
Particulars: Set of 2. Size is 1.5".

DATE:_____ $:_____
○ WISH ○ HAVE

'97
$11

Snowbabies™ Miniatures

Miniatures, How Much Longer?

In 1989, three years after the introduction of the porcelain Snowbabies™, the mini Snowbabies™ were born. These are made of pewter and are smaller, nearly exact replicas of their larger cousins. The first year of the minis produced 21 introductions in the line! Thankfully, the cost of these new Snowbabies™ was $7-$15. Still, there were certainly a lot of them. The fact that the names of the bisque and the pewter Snowbabies™ are the same has often proved to be confusing through the years. "Now which *Give Me A Push* are you talking about, the porcelain or the pewter?" You get the idea.

The introduction of the minis follows no specific pattern, though quite often the miniature version will be introduced the same year as the larger version. For example, the mini *Are All These Mine?* was introduced in the first year of this new mini line while the original porcelain version was introduced in the third year of the bisque Snowbabies™, so both were actually introduced in the same year. And most recently, the mini *You Need Wings Too!* was introduced in the same year as its larger cousin. As for the pewter retirements, they do not necessarily coincide with the bisque version and are announced in the same random fashion as any other Department 56 retirement.

Bisque Snowbabies™ and pewter Snowbabies™ have three things in common— they both eventually retire, they share the same designs, and they have the same names. Or do they? Look closely and you'll notice that they may not even have the designs and names in common. For example, the porcelain sign called *Polar Sign* will not be found in the smaller pewter version. Instead a similar design called *Collector Sign* is represented in the minis. Furthermore, in some cases, the miniature version will have pieces that can be removed from the main design. You can see this in the *Somewhere in Dreamland* and the *Penguin Parade* designs.

The porcelain Snowbabies™ took a while to catch on, and perhaps have never really reached the collectibility of the villages, but are a viable and sought after collectible by many Department 56® collectors. The same cannot be said of the minis. Part of the problem might be the large snow crystals that appeared on the Snowbabies™ suits in the early years. The pewter Snowbabies™ are so small that the snow on their suits was much too big for them. The snowflakes became a noticeable part of the design instead of just an enhancement. Then there was the problem of their being yellow, not a pretty yellow, but a dingy yellow. It seems as though these small pewter items yellowed with age. The minis have undergone a transformation with the recent year's productions having a more normal suit with small snowy specs. As for the yellowing, only time will tell.

Whatever the problems may be, the mini Snowbabies™ have never achieved the collectibility status of the porcelain ones. But maybe there are some ideas for the minis that don't require a collectible status. For instance, a secondary market broker recently stated that he always thought they were good for displaying in the North Pole™ collection. The minis are also an ideal collection for the younger members of families who are collecting the villages or larger porcelain Snowbabies™. They are small enough for little hands, they are not as easily broken (although they do break as he reminded me), and they are not as costly as most other Department 56® items. It gives youngsters a collection of their own and a lesson about the world of collectibles.

(continued on 106)

Snowbabies™ Miniatures

1996...

FIVE-PART HARMONY

ITEM #	INTRO	STATUS	OSRP	GBTru	NO
76710	1996	CURRENT	$22.00	**$22.00**	CHANGE

Product: Miniatures
Material: Pewter
Description: Snowbabies™ and Husky pup sing harmony.
Particulars: Set of 2. Size is 1.5".

DATE:_____ $:_____
○ WISH   ○ HAVE

'97
$22

HEIGH-HO, HEIGH-HO, TO FROLIC LAND WE GO!

ITEM #	INTRO	STATUS	OSRP	GBTru
76711	1997	CURRENT	$22.50	**$22.50**

Product: Miniature
Material: Pewter
Description: Four Snowbabies™ march to a tune played on a horn while carrying a tree.
Particulars: Size is 3" long.

DATE:_____ $:_____
○ WISH   ○ HAVE

Miniatures, How Much Longer?

(continued from 105)

More and more stores appear to be discontinuing their selling of this mini line. Canada's Department 56® distributor has chosen not to import any more of the miniature Snowbabies™. It has been cited that stores are not selling the product in quantities large enough to warrant importation.

So, where does this leave our littlest Snowbabies™ friends? It's uncertain for now. What is certain is that a company cannot continue to produce a line that is not well accepted. We have seen proof of this with the discontinuance of the Upstairs Downstairs Bears®, All Through The House™, and Merrymakers®. It wouldn't be a surprise if the miniature Snowbabies™ become one of Department 56, Inc.'s lines of the past.

the **Village Chronicle**.

Snowbabies™ Miniatures

WHISTLE WHILE YOU WORK

ITEM #	INTRO	STATUS	OSRP	GBTRU
76712	1997	CURRENT	$18.00	**$18.00**

Product: Miniature
Material: Pewter
Description: Snowbabies™ carry a shoulder-pole balancing a full kettle of stars.
Particulars: Size is 1.5".

DATE:_____ $:_____
○ WISH   ○ HAVE

JINGLE BELL

ITEM #	INTRO	STATUS	OSRP	GBTRU
76713	1997	CURRENT	$7.00	**$7.00**

Product: Miniature
Material: Pewter
Description: Snowbaby rings bell.
Particulars: Size is 1.5".

DATE:_____ $:_____
○ WISH   ○ HAVE

STARLIGHT SERENADE

ITEM #	INTRO	STATUS	OSRP	GBTRU
76714	1997	CURRENT	$12.00	**$12.00**

Product: Miniature
Material: Pewter
Description: Seated by a tree a Snowbaby plays mandolin underneath a dangling star.
Particulars: Size is 2".

DATE:_____ $:_____
○ WISH   ○ HAVE

THANK YOU

ITEM #	INTRO	STATUS	OSRP	GBTRU
76715	1997	CURRENT	$20.00	**$20.00**

Product: Miniatures
Material: Pewter
Description: Snowbaby receives gift from friend as they sit by candle-lit tree.
Particulars: Set of 3. Size is 2".

DATE:_____ $:_____
○ WISH   ○ HAVE

Snowbabies™ Miniatures

1997...

JACK FROST ... A TOUCH OF WINTER'S MAGIC

ITEM #	INTRO	STATUS	OSRP	GBTʀᴜ
76716	1997	CURRENT	$27.50	**$27.50**

Product: Miniatures
Material: Pewter
Description: Snowbaby, bear, puffin and penguins stand with Jack Frost as he frosts the stars.
Particulars: Set of 3. Size is 3".

DATE:_____ $:_____
○ WISH   ○ HAVE

WISH UPON A FALLING STAR

ITEM #	INTRO	STATUS	OSRP	GBTʀᴜ
76717	1997	CURRENT	$25.00	**$25.00**

Product: Miniatures
Material: Pewter
Description: Snowbaby riding polar bear spots falling stars through telescope. Snowbaby with husky pup plus two other Snowbabies™ make a wish as penguin and bunnies watch the stars.
Particulars: Set of 4. Size is 3".

DATE:_____ $:_____
○ WISH   ○ HAVE

BEST LITTLE STAR

ITEM #	INTRO	STATUS	OSRP	GBTʀᴜ
76718	1997	CURRENT	$6.50	**$6.50**

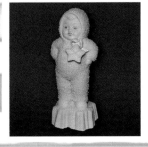

Product: Miniature
Material: Pewter
Description: Snowbaby wears a star on front of snowsuit.
Particulars: Size is 1.5".

DATE:_____ $:_____
○ WISH   ○ HAVE

*Notes:*_____
_____
_____
_____
_____
_____

Snowbabies™ Miniatures

Mercury Glass
The Night Before Christmas

Mercury Glass Ornaments are mouth-blown and hand painted. Each comes with a glass Snowbabies™ star linked with its own brass cap to the hanger. In addition, each has a tiny brass Department 56® Clock medallion attached. They are made in Poland.

SNOWBABY WITH WREATH

ITEM #	INTRO	STATUS	OSRP	GBTru	
68980	1996	CURRENT	$18.00	**$18.00**	NO CHANGE

Product: Ornament
Material: Mercury Glass, Brass Fittings
Description: Snowbaby with star wreath.
Particulars: Size is 5".

DATE:_____ $:_____

○ WISH   ○ HAVE

'97
$18

SNOWBABY ON PACKAGE

ITEM #	INTRO	STATUS	OSRP	GBTru	
68981	1996	CURRENT	$18.00	**$18.00**	NO CHANGE

Product: Ornament
Material: Mercury Glass, Brass Fittings
Description: Snowbaby stands on a package.
Particulars: Size is 5".

DATE:_____ $:_____

○ WISH   ○ HAVE

'97
$18

SNOWBABY SOLDIER

ITEM #	INTRO	STATUS	OSRP	GBTRU	NO
68982	1996	CURRENT	$18.00	**$18.00**	CHANGE

Product: Ornament
Material: Mercury Glass, Brass Fittings
Description: Snowbaby soldier.
Particulars: Size is 5".

DATE:_____ $:_____
○ WISH   ○ HAVE

'97
$18

SNOWBABY DRUMMER

ITEM #	INTRO	STATUS	OSRP	GBTRU	NO
68983	1996	CURRENT	$18.00	**$18.00**	CHANGE

Product: Ornament
Material: Mercury Glass, Brass Fittings
Description: Snowbaby drummer.
Particulars: Size is 5".

DATE:_____ $:_____
○ WISH   ○ HAVE

'97
$18

SNOWBABY ON SNOWBALL

ITEM #	INTRO	STATUS	OSRP	GBTRU	NO
68984	1996	CURRENT	$20.00	**$20.00**	CHANGE

Product: Ornament
Material: Mercury Glass, Brass Fittings
Description: Snowbaby on snowball.
Particulars: Size is 4.5".

DATE:_____ $:_____
○ WISH   ○ HAVE

'97
$20

SNOWBABY IN PACKAGE

ITEM #	INTRO	STATUS	OSRP	GBTRU	NO
68986	1996	CURRENT	$18.00	**$18.00**	CHANGE

Product: Ornament
Material: Mercury Glass, Brass Fittings
Description: Snowbaby in package.
Particulars: Size is 5".

DATE:_____ $:_____
○ WISH   ○ HAVE

'97
$18

SNOWBABY WITH BELL

ITEM #	INTRO	STATUS	OSRP	GBTRU	NO
68987	1996	CURRENT	$18.00	**$18.00**	CHANGE

Product: Ornament
Material: Mercury Glass, Brass Fittings
Description: Snowbaby with bell.
Particulars: Size is 3.25", 2.5".

DATE:_____ $:_____
○ WISH   ○ HAVE

'97
$18

SNOWBABY ON MOON

ITEM #	INTRO	STATUS	OSRP	GBTRU	NO
68988	1996	CURRENT	$18.00	**$18.00**	CHANGE

Product: Ornament
Material: Mercury Glass, Brass Fittings
Description: Snowbaby on moon.
Particulars: Size is 5".

DATE:_____ $:_____
○ WISH   ○ HAVE

'97
$18

SNOWBABY JINGLEBABY

ITEM #	INTRO	STATUS	OSRP	GBTRU	NO
68989	1996	CURRENT	$20.00	**$20.00**	CHANGE

Product: Ornament
Material: Mercury Glass, Brass Fittings
Description: Snowbaby jinglebaby.
Particulars: Size is 4.25".

DATE:_____ $:_____
○ WISH   ○ HAVE

'97
$20

SNOWBABY WITH TREE

ITEM #	INTRO	STATUS	OSRP	GBTRU	NO
68990	1996	CURRENT	$20.00	**$20.00**	CHANGE

Product: Ornament
Material: Mercury Glass, Brass Fittings
Description: Snowbaby with sisal tree.
Particulars: Size is 4.5".

DATE:_____ $:_____
○ WISH   ○ HAVE

'97
$20

Snowbabies™ Mercury Glass

Snowbaby With Star

Item #	Intro	Status	OSRP	GBTru	
68991	1996	Current	$18.00	**$18.00**	NO CHANGE

Product: Ornament
Material: Mercury Glass, Brass Fittings
Description: Snowbaby with star.
Particulars: Size is 5".

DATE:_____ $:_____

○ WISH   ○ HAVE

'97
$18

Snowbaby On Tree

Item #	Intro	Status	OSRP	GBTru
68992	1997	Current	$22.50	**$22.50**

Product: Ornament
Material: Mercury Glass, Brass Fittings
Description: Snowbaby holds a star and stands atop a tree.
Particulars: Midyear release.

DATE:_____ $:_____

○ WISH   ○ HAVE

Snowbaby On Drum

Item #	Intro	Status	OSRP	GBTru
68993	1997	Current	$22.50	**$22.50**

Product: Ornament
Material: Mercury Glass, Brass Fittings
Description: Snowbaby plays a concertina while standing on a drum.
Particulars: Midyear release.

DATE:_____ $:_____

○ WISH   ○ HAVE

Snowbaby In Stocking

Item #	Intro	Status	OSRP	GBTru
68994	1997	Current	$20.00	**$20.00**

Product: Ornament
Material: Mercury Glass, Brass Fittings
Description: Snowbaby in Stocking.

DATE:_____ $:_____

○ WISH   ○ HAVE

Snowbabies™ Mercury Glass

Snowbaby On Skis

Item #	Intro	Status	OSRP	GBTru
68995	1997	Current	$20.00	**$20.00**

Product: Ornament
Material: Mercury Glass, Brass Fittings
Description: Snowbaby on skis.

DATE:_____ $:_____
○ WISH ○ HAVE

Snowbaby In Skate

Item #	Intro	Status	OSRP	GBTru
68996	1997	Current	$20.00	**$20.00**

Product: Ornament
Material: Mercury Glass, Brass Fittings
Description: Snowbaby in skate.

DATE:_____ $:_____
○ WISH ○ HAVE

Snowbaby Angel

Item #	Intro	Status	OSRP	GBTru
68997	1997	Current	$18.00	**$18.00**

Product: Ornament
Material: Mercury Glass, Brass Fittings
Description: Snowbaby as angel.

DATE:_____ $:_____
○ WISH ○ HAVE

Snowbaby Jack Frost

Item #	Intro	Status	OSRP	GBTru
68998	1997	Current	$37.50	**$37.50**

Product: Ornament
Material: Mercury Glass, Brass Fittings
Description: Snowbaby as Jack Frost.

DATE:_____ $:_____
○ WISH ○ HAVE

Snowbabies™ Mercury Glass

OTHER GUIDES FROM GREENBOOK

GREENBOOK Guide to
> The Enesco Precious Moments Collection

GREENBOOK Guide to
> Department 56® Villages including
> The Original Snow Village® and
> The Heritage Village Collection®

GREENBOOK Guide to
> Ty® Beanie Babies™

GREENBOOK Guide to
> Hallmark Keepsake Ornaments

GREENBOOK Guide to
> Hallmark Kiddie Car Classics

GREENBOOK Guide to
> The Walt Disney Classics Collection

GREENBOOK Guide to
> Cherished Teddies by Enesco

GREENBOOK Guide to
> Precious Moments Company Dolls

GREENBOOK Guide to
> Harbour Lights

GREENBOOK Guide to
> Boyds Bears

GREENBOOK Guide to
> Charming Tails

Snowbabies Friendship Club™ Particulars

- Members who joined between December 5, 1997 and January 31, 1998* are Charter Members. Charter Members received a special charter charm (bar with words "charter member"), in addition to the 1998 membership charm (star with 1998 printed on it), and a special indication is made on the membership card and certificate.

Snowbabies
FRIENDSHIP CLUB™

- The Membership Kit, #68851, SRP $35, contains the following:
    - Welcome Gift, "You Better Watch Out" figurine
    - Mechanical illustration of the Club Redemption Piece, "Together We Can Make The Season Bright" signed by the artist with a special Snowbabies™ frame
    - Snowbabies™ Friendship Pin that will hold charms to be distributed throughout membership

- The second part of the Kit contains personalized items. Once membership has been processed, the collector receives a Welcome Packet in the mail that contains:
    - A personalized membership card with name, membership number, and membership start month
    - Membership certificate
    - Membership charm to be attached to Friendship Pin
    - A voucher that entitles member to purchase the exclusive Club Redemption Piece

- Members will also receive a newsletter twice a year.

*Department 56, Inc. extended the Charter Membership period an additional two weeks after the 1/31/98 original cutoff date.

To contact the Club:

Snowbabies Friendship Club™
PO Box 44656
Eden Prairie, MN   55344-2356
1-888-SNOWBABY (1-888-766-9222)

QuikReference

Welcome Gift

68851 .... 1997/8 .. You Better Watch Out!

Redemption Piece

68852 .... 1997/8 .. Together We Can Make The Season Bright

Charms

1997/8 .. Charter Members Bar
1997/8 .. Star

Snowbabies Friendship Club™

FRIENDSHIP CLUB MEMBERSHIP KIT	ITEM # 68851	INTRO 1997	STATUS MEMBER ONLY– WELCOME GIFT	OSRP $35.00	GBTRU $35.00

Product: Figurine, Pin & Illustration

Description: Set of 6 contains the Membership Kit figurine, "You Better Watch Out," a mechanical illustration of the redemption piece signed by artist Kristi Jensen Pierro with a special Snowbabies™ frame, a Snowbabies™ Friendship Pin that will hold charms distributed throughout collector's membership. Second part of kit is personalized items mailed under separate cover: membership card, membership certificate, voucher for purchasing the redemption piece and charm to be attached to Friendship Pin.

Particulars: Photo to the left is a close-up of "You Better Watch Out" — a Snowbaby warns penguin to be careful as tree tips as star is placed on top.

DATE:_____ $:_____
○ WISH   ○ HAVE

TOGETHER WE CAN MAKE THE SEASON BRIGHT	ITEM # 68852	INTRO 1997	STATUS MEMBER ONLY– REDEMPTION PIECE	OSRP $75.00	GBTRU $75.00

Product: Figurine
Material: Porcelain
Description: Little girl adds shining star to top of a frosty pine tree too high for the Snowbabies™ to reach.
Particulars: Club redemption figurine features a new Snowbabies™ Snowfriend–the little girl from the book, "Winter Tales of the Snowbabies," a collection of legends and poems about the Snowbabies™ and their tiny friends. This little girl will only be featured in Snowbabies Friendship Club™ exclusive designs. Size is 8.5".

DATE:_____ $:_____
○ WISH   ○ HAVE

Snowbabies Friendship Club™

Number Index

117

Snowbabies™

Snowbabies™ Name Index

Miniatures

Snowbabies™/Miniatures Name Index 119

Mercury Glass

Friendship Club